Body Image and Self-Esteem

ISSUES

Volume 170

Series Editor

Lisa Firth

Independence

Educational Publishers
Cambridge

First published by Independence
The Studio, High Green
Great Shelford
Cambridge CB22 5EG
England

© Independence 2009

British Library Cataloguing in Publication Data
Body Image and Self-Esteem – (Issues; v. 170)
1. Self-esteem 2. Body image
I. Series II. Firth, Lisa
158.1-dc22

ISBN-13: 978 1 86168 484 4

Printed in Great Britain
MWL Print Group Ltd

Cover
The illustration on the front cover is by
Don Hatcher.

CONTENTS

Chapter One: Self-Esteem

Chapter Two: Body Image

Useful information for readers

Dear Reader,

Issues: Body Image and Self-Esteem

Most people will suffer from low self-esteem at some point in their lives. We might worry about the way we look, academic or career performance, how others perceive us and the shape of our bodies. This book looks at issues surrounding positive self-image, self-respect and confidence. It also addresses our relationship with our bodies, media pressures to maintain a certain body shape and the rise of cosmetic surgery.

The purpose of Issues

Body Image and Self-Esteem is the one hundred and seventieth volume in the **Issues** series. The aim of this series is to offer up-to-date information about important issues in our world. Whether you are a regular reader or new to the series, we do hope you find this book a useful overview of the many and complex issues involved in the topic. This title replaces an older volume in the **Issues** series, Volume 117: **Self-Esteem and Body Image,** which is now out of print.

Titles in the **Issues** series are resource books designed to be of especial use to those undertaking project work or requiring an overview of facts, opinions and information on a particular subject, particularly as a prelude to undertaking their own research.

The information in this book is not from a single author, publication or organisation; the value of this unique series lies in the fact that it presents information from a wide variety of sources, including:
⇨ Government reports and statistics
⇨ Newspaper articles and features
⇨ Information from think-tanks and policy institutes
⇨ Magazine features and surveys
⇨ Website material
⇨ Literature from lobby groups and charitable organisations.*

Critical evaluation

Because the information reprinted here is from a number of different sources, readers should bear in mind the origin of the text and whether the source is likely to have a particular bias or agenda when presenting information (just as they would if undertaking their own research). It is hoped that, as you read about the many aspects of the issues explored in this book, you will critically evaluate the information presented. It is important that you decide whether you are being presented with facts or opinions. Does the writer give a biased or an unbiased report? If an opinion is being expressed, do you agree with the writer?

Body Image and Self-Esteem offers a useful starting point for those who need convenient access to information about the many issues involved. However, it is only a starting point. Following each article is a URL to the relevant organisation's website, which you may wish to visit for further information.

Kind regards,

Lisa Firth
Editor, **Issues** series

Please note that Independence Publishers has no political affiliations or opinions on the topics covered in the Issues series, and any views quoted in this book are not necessarily those of the publisher or its staff.

ISSUES TODAY
A RESOURCE FOR KEY STAGE 3

Younger readers can also now benefit from the thorough editorial process which characterises the **Issues** series with the launch of a new range of titles for 11- to 14-year-old students, **Issues Today**. In addition to containing information from a wide range of sources, rewritten with this age group in mind, **Issues Today** titles also feature comprehensive glossaries, an accessible and attractive layout and handy tasks and assignments which can be used in class, for homework or as a revision aid. In addition, these titles are fully photocopiable. For more information, please visit the **Issues Today** section of our website (www.independence. co.uk).

What is self-esteem?

Information from Shining Bright

We are all familiar with the expression 'self-esteem' – but what does it really mean? The word 'esteem' is derived from the Latin word which means 'to estimate'. As such, identifying whether or not we are suffering from low or high self-esteem can be established by focusing on how we 'estimate' or view ourselves.

It is human nature for us to compare ourselves to others and we may measure achievements, lifestyle, relationships and many other factors against people we interact with. This can be within our own peer groups or at work. This helps us to confirm our position in life and how we respond to these factors can denote our level of self-esteem. Our self-worth is usually based on our previous performances. Our own personal values tend to be based on how successfully we believe that we have performed in a variety of different situations – unfortunately, we often expect perfect performance from ourselves. When we don't match up to these expectations, for whatever reason, we tend to lower our own self-values.

We are also greatly influenced by a society which demands high standards and flawless performance and this can contribute to us losing sight of the fact that making mistakes is a part of life and should not have a negative impact on how we view ourselves. It is natural to care about how we perform, but it is more important that we are able to like and love ourselves for who we are. As children, we never questioned our self confidence, we tended to take people at face value without searching for signs of failure. Sadly, as we grow older we find ourselves continually justifying our worth and social standing and becoming obsessed with not being perfect.

By relying on the approval of others we are placing all of our own value in someone else's hands, which means that our self-confidence and self-esteem are effectively out of our control. Control is an important issue in relation to self-esteem and makes us totally dependant on how someone else reacts towards us or feels about us. This can leave us feeling vulnerable and we should avoid doing this wherever possible. It is always important to remember the qualities in ourselves that we value, as this helps maintain self-worth and confidence. Close friends can often provide value in this way – if you trust someone and can discuss positive and negative thoughts, it can draw us closer to our valuable attributes.

It is natural to care about how we perform, but it is more important that we are able to like and love ourselves for who we are

---

Failing at something can create feelings of frustration and inadequacy. Feeling like this for even a short period of time can chip away at self confidence and self-worth. One proven method of maintaining self-confidence is to make a list of things that we know we do well and doing one of these things each day. This reaffirms our self-belief and also generates a level of pride that we are able to complete a task frequently. Making a list of 'likeable' qualities can help us rediscover the aspects of our personality that get taken for granted or forgotten in day-to-day living. 'Private time' is another way of taking time out for ourselves. Pampering yourself or doing something you enjoy creates feelings of positivity. We can also treat our friends and show them the same level of care. Pushing our existing boundaries is another way to increase self-confidence. There may be things that we have always wanted to do but have never risked it or taken up the challenge, however small it may seem. Accepting a challenge can have really positive effects on our self-confidence – even if we fail.

Genuine self-belief plays a strong part in this overall process and this comes from within. This is about recognising imperfections and knowing limitations, but also being able to celebrate our strengths and work towards achievable goals. Any of us should be able to shine and take responsibility for ourselves, our actions and our behaviours. In doing this, we can work towards achieving a balanced, happy and successful life and truly believing that we deserve the best that life has to offer.

If you have already tried to do some of these things and are still concerned about your self-confidence and worth, it is important to remember that it is natural for us to experience temporary fluctuations – this happens to most of us. However, if our moods seem to shift on a regular basis or our self confidence is low for a period of time, it is important to seek professional help. Sometimes we find that we lack the necessary 'foundations' upon which to develop strong personal self-image. This is something we at 'Shining Bright' may be able to help you with. If you were to contact us, you can be assured that we will be happy to talk with you about your concerns, in confidence and design a special program adapted to your needs.

⇨ The above information is reprinted with kind permission from Shining Bright. Visit www.shining-bright.co.uk for more information.

© Shining Bright

Self-esteem

Information from beat

Self-esteem can be described as the way we feel about ourselves, how we value ourselves or how much we like ourselves.

This definition comes from *The Self-Esteem Directory*:

'Self-esteem is a person's unconditional appreciation of her/himself. It matters because people who do not value themselves feel unworthy. They can then treat themselves and others badly, usually unintentionally. Low self-esteem is often a major factor in abuse, depression, crime, loneliness, low achievement, addiction, mental illness and unhappiness.'

The unconditional aspect of self-esteem is really important

If we accept ourselves without 'conditions' we can accept praise or criticism without it badly affecting our sense of self-worth.

It also means we have realistic expectations of ourselves, with a clear view of our strengths and weaknesses.

We are no longer dependent on other people's view of ourselves. This is why self-esteem is so important for learning. If we can trust ourselves we can take the risk of making a mistake.

Unconditional appreciation of ourselves means accepting ourselves as we are, including our body, our feelings and our abilities. It means going beyond 'image' and recognising our fundamental worth as a human being.

In other words, recognising our abil-ity to love, experience joy, communicate and be creative, as well as acknowledging that we can be lazy, destructive or cruel. By appreciating both our negative and positive aspects we take responsibility for ourselves and grow.

Low self-esteem

These are some of the feelings and attitudes involved:
- dependency;
- feeling helpless and needing approval;
- hostility towards others;
- feelings of apathy, of being powerless, isolation, not worth loving;
- withdrawal;
- too keen to please and follow others;
- depression;
- anxiety;
- preferring to give in;
- poor general health;
- tendency to criticise and be negative about other people;
- if you feel negative about yourself, you tend to think everyone else does too.

Self-esteem cannot be permanently raised by changing your appearance – it is simply tackling the problem at the wrong level, on the outside, rather than the inside of the person and how she/he really feels about themselves.

We downgrade our self-esteem by

- Emphasising what we did not achieve, rather than what we did;
- spending more time talking about our mistakes, rather than what we got right;
- trivialising our skills, knowledge or gifts;
- giving more importance to other's criticisms than compliments;
- giving credit to others not ourselves;
- putting ourselves down.

Re-energising self-esteem

- Be good to yourself and treat yourself as special – try to remember you are worthy;
- talk to others you trust about the things you find difficult and allow yourself to express difficult and negative feelings;
- we all have our dreams and the right to dream them;
- identify what you're good at and give yourself praise for it;
- try to remember other people have needs too.

Self-esteem is the most precious gift you have – treasure it and yourself.
23 January 2009

- The above information is reprinted with kind permission from beat. Visit www.b-eat.co.uk for more information.

© beat

Do you sometimes wish you were someone else?

Information from Care for the Family

Julia had struggled with the way she looked ever since the day her mother said, 'You might not be as good-looking as your sister, but at least you've got a good brain'. Her mother's motive was to encourage her, but the insensitive remark didn't help; Julia grew up believing she was ugly. And when all her college friends had boyfriends and she didn't, she believed that even more.

John looked at the pile of papers on his office desk. He felt quite out of his depth. Looking round the office, he saw everyone else busy working at their computers or speaking confidently on the phone. He felt he'd be out of a job if he couldn't sort himself out soon. Ah well, he thought, his teacher certainly knew what she was talking about when she'd said 'You'll never come to much'.

Those feelings of inadequacy, of other people being better than we are, of believing that we're no good, are sure signs of a lack of self-esteem.

Uphill struggle

Most of us struggle with this concept of self. Perhaps all your friends have been to university and you never did. Or you think 'everyone else' is more popular or prettier or more confident. It could be that you were brought up by parents who gave you the message that you were not special or worthy of being cared for, so learning to believe in yourself is an uphill struggle.

Having good self-esteem doesn't mean being arrogant or big-headed; it's about believing in yourself, and knowing that although you might not be perfect, you're still a valuable, unique human being. It's about having self-worth and being confident in the person you are, so that you don't have to feel diminished by others' accomplishments.

Good self-esteem doesn't only benefit you; it also enables you to

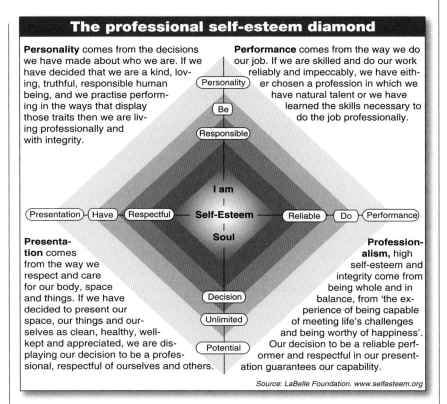

The professional self-esteem diamond

Personality comes from the decisions we have made about who we are. If we have decided that we are a kind, loving, truthful, responsible human being, and we practise performing in the ways that display those traits then we are living professionally and with integrity.

Performance comes from the way we do our job. If we are skilled and do our work reliably and impeccably, we have either chosen a profession in which we have natural talent or we have learned the skills necessary to do the job professionally.

Personality — Be — Responsible

I am — Self-Esteem — Soul

Presentation — Have — Respectful — Reliable — Do — Performance

Decision — Unlimited — Potential

Presentation comes from the way we respect and care for our body, space and things. If we have decided to present our space, our things and ourselves as clean, healthy, well-kept and appreciated, we are displaying our decision to be a professional, respectful of ourselves and others.

Professionalism, high self-esteem and integrity come from being whole and in balance, from 'the experience of being capable of meeting life's challenges and being worthy of happiness'. Our decision to be a reliable performer and respectful in our presentation guarantees our capability.

Source: LaBelle Foundation. www.selfesteem.org

maintain good relationships with others. When you constantly feel inadequate, it can be difficult to accept constructive criticism or admit to being in the wrong. It also means that you don't feel the need to put other people down in order to bolster yourself up.

When you lack self-esteem, a destructive cycle of thought begins: 'It's not surprising things are going wrong for me because I'm dull/unattractive/not clever... therefore no-one likes me... nothing will ever go right... I won't get a good job... so what's the point of making the effort?'

What can you do to prevent this cycle of thought in yourself?
⇨ Focus on the truth that you are a valuable, unique human being, who is deserving of good things.
⇨ Don't compare yourself to others; everyone has their own gifts and talents.
⇨ 'Don't go there.' When the

negative thoughts start, sometimes it's necessary to nip them in the bud straight away, to stop it from becoming a downward spiral.
⇨ List your accomplishments, making sure you include those that you have taken for granted. Choose to put out of your mind those negative feelings that tell you that your friends' accomplishments are greater than yours.
⇨ Pat yourself on the back when you've done a good job.
⇨ It may be that you're feeling tired and depressed, and you ignore your own needs. Give yourself some attention – some 'you time'. You need to keep your battery topped up so that you can continue to give to others!

⇨ The above information is reprinted with kind permission from Care for the Family. Visit www.careforthefamily.org.uk for more.
© Care for the Family

How do you really feel about yourself?

Information from the Dove Self-Esteem Fund

Choose the answer that MOST represents how you feel or behave NOW. Don't answer as you would like to be or have been in the past. Answer the best you can about how you are now.

1. When I meet new people at a party:
a) I say 'hi' and if I can, I quickly make an excuse to leave.
b) I try hard to look them in the eye and make conversation, even though I feel awkward.
c) I am curious and interested in the other person and like to explore our common and different interests.

2. When I try something new and it doesn't work out:
a) I keep thinking what an idiot I am, long after the event.
b) I feel bad, but then I move onto something that I know I can do.
c) I look at what went wrong, and how I could do it better, and if I have the opportunity, I try again.

3. A friend keeps breaking a date with me:
a) I believe that she doesn't want to be friends with me anymore and I stop calling her.
b) I feel hurt, especially as she still seems to be seeing other people, so I call and ask what I've done wrong.
c) I call her and ask what's happening, and is she okay?

4. An argument starts between two of my friends:
a) I don't want either to not like me, so I say that I don't have an opinion on the matter.
b) I try to act as peacemaker by saying each of them is right in part.
c) I say what I think about the situation without being personal about their points of view.

5. When planning an outing, if I want to do something that the others in my group don't:
a) I give in quickly because they're probably right that it wouldn't be fun.
b) I argue that I never get to do what I want, until they give in.
c) I see if we can compromise so that we do make plans to do my thing another day.

6. When I hear my voice talking to myself in my head:
a) I am usually putting myself down and being emotionally punitive.
b) I can be pretty critical but mostly I am telling myself that I did okay.
c) I am mostly very positive about what I do and how I feel. Even when things have gone badly I won't let myself say bad things about myself.

7. I have decided to make a commitment to doing something for myself:
a) It doesn't take me long to break my commitment to myself and find myself doing the same old things, especially for other people.
b) I start with some anxiety about not doing it well, and if it gets really hard, I might quit.
c) I stick to it. I understand that it will take me a while to learn something new and believe that the effort and mistakes will be worth it in the end.

8. When someone tells me what they think about me or what I do:
a) I feel attacked and feel very hurt, even if they are saying it nicely.
b) I get defensive, explaining why I do things the way that I do. I might also turn it back onto them and their behaviour.
c) I listen to what they say, and if it seems right to me, or important, I think about how to make positive changes in myself.

9. Looking at myself in the mirror:
a) You're kidding! I try NOT to look. I'm unattractive and insecure.
b) I think that I am pretty average, and can work on a number of things.
c) I mostly feel attractive and confident about myself.

10. When I get up in the morning:
a) I pull on whatever clothes are at hand and drag myself into the day.
b) I try on a few outfits before feeling that I can successfully face the day.
c) I know that all my clothes suit me, so I reach for what is appropriate for my day's activities.

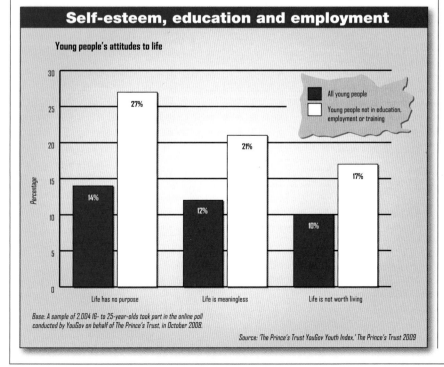

Self-esteem, education and employment

Young people's attitudes to life

- All young people
- Young people not in education, employment or training

Base: A sample of 2,004 16- to 25-year-olds took part in the online poll conducted by YouGov on behalf of The Prince's Trust, in October 2008.

Source: 'The Prince's Trust YouGov Youth Index.' The Prince's Trust 2009

Mostly As

Time to turn the tables

We all have something that we are good at, and you're no exception.

However, you seem to be very hard on yourself and always look at what you did wrong or can't do. In other words, you're really good at seeing the down side.

Now is a good time to turn that around and see what you do well. You need some strategies to begin to believe in your ability to make good choices and to do well. Start by taking responsibility for your actions and your feelings. Question whether there is a more positive way of interpreting events, and reacting to them. It is amazing how powerful we can feel when we know that we have control over how we choose to respond.

We all have something that we are good at, and you're no exception

---

Mostly Bs

Taking more risk could help your self-esteem

It sounds like most days you feel okay about yourself, but there is still a wide thread of self-criticism that undermines your self-confidence. Perhaps it is time for you to take more risks. Each time we try something new and succeed, we feel more competent and better about ourselves.

You could also benefit from looking at how you think about yourself and your life. What is realistic and what can you change? Don't limit yourself to how you think about yourself now. Just because you don't feel you are able to do something specific now, doesn't mean you won't be able to in a day, a week, or... whenever.

Lastly, try to take yourself less seriously and have some fun!

Mostly Cs

You have good self-esteem!

It sounds like you really know – and like – who you are.

There is a lot of positive self-worth that comes from knowing you are able to make good choices even if you don't always do so. It also seems like you are able to accept responsibility for your actions and look a the positive side of life.

Don't forget to keep your self-confidence high by speaking well to yourself and of yourself. It's important to not allow others to put you down. It's clear that you can also be a great role model to your family, friends and colleagues. You can show them how important healthy self-esteem is just by knowing that you are capable of making good choices and living well.

⇨ The above information is reprinted with kind permission from the Dove Self-Esteem Fund. Visit http://campaignforrealbeauty.co.uk for more information on building self-esteem.

© Dove Self-Esteem Fund

'Soft skills' for low self-esteem

Information from Uncommon Knowledge

Learning sports, languages and practical skills like driving or carpentry can all raise a sense of competency. However, handling our emotions effectively is also a skill. Emotional skills are sometimes termed 'soft skills'.

Some of these soft skills include:

⇨ Being able to 'read' the emotions of others.
⇨ Knowing when others are angry, upset, unsettled etc.
⇨ Being sensitive to others whilst realising that we, too, have a position within any given situation.
⇨ Having empathy. Being able to put ourselves in the position of the other person.
⇨ Being able to assert our point of view. When appropriate speaking up for ourselves assertively.
⇨ Having an effective communication style.
⇨ Being able to make ourselves understood and being able to compromise to the benefit of all involved.
⇨ Having good rapport skills and being able to forge and maintain friendships.
⇨ Observing our own emotional ebbs and flows.
⇨ Knowing how to manage our own anger and 'low times' so we are not swamped by our own emotions.
⇨ Understanding our own needs for company, rest, creative stimulation, healthy lifestyle, achievable goals and attention and intimacy, so that we can feel a sense of control.
⇨ Making allowances for these needs in our everyday life.
⇨ Having wide interests and activities (as far as possible). So we are not just 'Mother', 'Wife', 'Co-worker', 'Father', etc.
⇨ Being able to manage stress in our lives – which relates to some of the above skills.
⇨ Understanding the paramount importance of the company we keep. Do we just mix with people who bring us down, or do we associate with others who are positive and fun?

A person's self-esteem seems to match the extent to which they have the above skills in place.

⇨ The above information is reprinted with kind permission from www.self-confidence.co.uk and Uncommon Knowledge. Visit www.uncommon-knowledge.co.uk for more information.

© Uncommon Knowledge

Recognise your negative thinking patterns

Information from MSN

Do you automatically think 'I'm useless' if you do something wrong, or assume that if your neighbour ignores you, she must hate you?

These distorted thoughts can really take their toll on your self-esteem. Below is a list of 10 negative ways of thinking. If you can recognise yourself having these thoughts, then you can begin the process of rationalising them.

1. Personalisation
Even though it's largely out of your control you blame yourself for a negative event that occurred: 'If I had taken more care, I never would have lost my mobile phone.'

2. Filtering
One negative happening, such as a rude comment made to you during an otherwise enjoyable evening, changes your whole perspective on the evening and puts you on a downer.

3. Rejecting praise
Closing off the positive, such as a compliment, affectionate gesture or praise, which goes unnoticed, ignored or deflected; you might reply with, 'It's no big deal.'

4. Drawing false conclusions
You draw negative conclusions without getting your facts straight. You try and predict the future or guess what someone else is feeling: 'My sister is upset, she must be angry with me.'

5. Negative reasoning
You are sure that your negative opinion of a situation reflects reality. Such as: 'My husband drops his socks on the floor just to aggravate me.'

6. Using the word 'should' in your vocabulary
You adhere to being a perfectionist and following certain rules about what you 'should' be doing. You feel useless and guilty when you can't stick to your rules.

7. Overgeneralisation
One negative event, such as an insult from your partner or an argument with someone, causes you to exaggerate the situation. For example, you might think, 'She's always cold' or 'You can't trust anyone.'

Negative thoughts don't have to be a way of life; you can 'unlearn' self-defeating ways of thinking

---

8. Labelling
Rather than learning from a mistake and using it as an experience that has helped you grow as a person, you label yourself negatively: 'I'm a failure'. You do the same to other people too: 'She's so controlling'.

9. Magnification or minimisation
You wind yourself up so that molehill problems become mountains: 'I know I won't be any good at it'. Or you minimize anything that might make you feel good, such as appreciation for a kind act you did or the recognition that other people have flaws, too.

10. All or nothing
If you don't perform with perfection, then you consider yourself a complete failure.

Negative thoughts don't have to be a way of life; you can 'unlearn' self-defeating ways of thinking that pave the way toward mood disorders.

Writing things down on paper really helps. Take some time out of your day to write down a negative event, notice your thought pattern from the list above and then write down a different perspective with a more rational and optimistic response.

Just the act of writing gives you back some power and control over the situation and once you have recognised your negative thought pattern you are on the way to teaching yourself new patterns – positive ones!

⇨ The above information is reprinted with kind permission from MSN. Visit http://style.uk.msn.com for more information.

© MSN

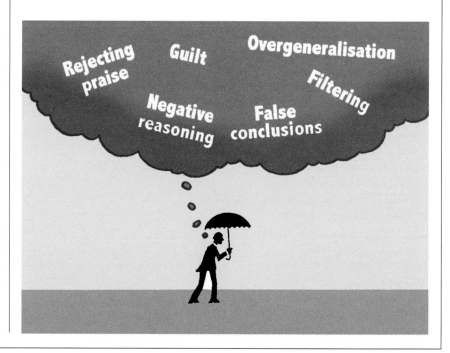

Learn how to be your own best friend

Switch off the critical voice and be kinder to yourself

By Lesley Garner

I have this person who follows me about all day, hurling insults. 'Idiot!' she exclaims when I delete the wrong email.

'No willpower,' she sneers, when I order an extra glass of wine or succumb to the dessert I'd told myself I was going to turn down. 'Lazybones!' she shrieks, if I turn over for an extra five minutes in bed.

It's very wearing, this constant barrage of undermining putdowns and curses. And, oddly enough, despite this person being so severe and critical, she doesn't succeed in making me modify my behaviour.

She certainly doesn't build up my confidence or make me feel good about myself in any way. And yet I find it very hard to shake her off.

Compare her with my real best friends – luckily I have quite a few. These wonderful men and women tell me I look great when I've made an effort to look good – after this other person has looked me up and down with scorn.

They tell me I'm doing a great job when this other person despairs of my ever getting it right. They listen to my woes without agreeing with her that I have every reason to doubt myself. They tell me to relax, that I'm being too hard on myself. They remind me of things I have done that worked, of places I've been that made me happy.

I associate them with good times and bright visions, while this other person only ever reminds me of failures and broken dreams.

The thing is, this other person is me. She is an agglomerate of all the negative judgments, midnight terrors and critical harshness that I have ever experienced. And the really mad thing is that she is the one I listen to.

When she has control over my brain, I can take the kindest compliment and crush it under foot. 'Oh, you're only saying that to cheer me up,' I think. And what, exactly, is wrong with that?

Most of us, unless we are lucky enough to be fantastically optimistic, carry this dark critic inside us, and one of the arts of living well is to notice it and turn down the volume. In order to be happy and successful, we need to replace this corrosive onslaught with the kinder voices that offer us patience and encouragement.

We can learn to correct the harshness and become our own best friend

Imagine that you are taking care of a small child. Unless you are some Dickensian villain, you do not attack this small person's confidence with withering criticism. If a child spills something, you laugh if off, saying that it's only an accident.

You try to minimise his distress. When he draws a picture you find something to love about it. When he feels shy or unhappy, you cuddle and tease and coax him. Why can't we behave in this essentially kind way towards our own selves?

The dark side of each of us, this withering inner voice, can be challenged and replaced with something more merciful and more nurturing. If we pay attention to the way we talk to ourselves in private we can learn to correct the harshness and become our own best friend.

This isn't New Age twaddle, it's a way of changing the quality of our lives. It doesn't mean that you cease being self-critical - we need to be self-critical in order to improve - but

it does mean we learn sometimes to hold back on the insults and give ourselves a pat on the back.

Think of the kindest person you know, the most encouraging teacher or the most loving mother. It's their voice you want to keep in your head.

When you make a mess of a task, don't shout at yourself and hurl insults. Sit back. Tell yourself that you haven't got it right this time, but congratulate yourself for trying.

Then suggest to yourself that you have another go, maybe trying something differently. Tell yourself that you know you can do it and gently remind yourself of some past success.

And finally, if you really want to see your inner monster for what it is, take a piece of paper and write down, without pausing to think, all the rude, destructive and negative things you hurl at yourself in your own mind.

Would you give houseroom to this person in real life? Of course not. It's time to get them right out of your head for ever.

8 November 2008

Confidence and self-esteem

Information from the University of Wolverhampton

Confidence and self-esteem are intangible and therefore a little difficult to define precisely. They describe an internal state, made up of what we think and feel about ourselves. This state is changeable according to the situation we are currently in and our responses to events going on around us. It is not unusual to feel quite confident in some circumstances and very under-confident in others. It is also influenced by past events and how we remember them; recalling a former success has a very different result in terms of our confidence levels than does bringing to mind an occasion when we failed.

Confidence and self-esteem are terms which are often used interchangeably, but although there is overlap, perhaps there are subtle differences. Confidence can refer to how we feel about ourselves and our abilities, whereas self-esteem refers directly to whether or not we appreciate and value ourselves. We may have been discouraged about being boastful, but a healthy amount of self-liking and self-approval is necessary if we are to have the confidence to meet life's challenges and participate as fully as we wish to in whatever makes life enjoyable and rewarding for us. In a sense, we could say that having self-esteem leads to being confident.

Where do self-esteem and confidence come from?

Early experiences are probably very influential in determining whether we achieve a healthy level of self-esteem. Experiences which help us to develop self-esteem include:
⇨ Being loved even when we do something wrong.
⇨ Being praised for our efforts.
⇨ Being encouraged to do new things.
⇨ Being offered the appropriate level of support – too much may encourage us to doubt ourselves –

too little may deter us from trying anything or allow us to attempt something which is beyond us.
⇨ Being given responsibility appropriate to our age and abilities.
⇨ Being given appropriate and consistent guidance.

Experiences which are likely to damage our self-esteem include:
⇨ Inconsistent demands and expectations.
⇨ Being criticised (when the criticism is unjustified or not constructive).
⇨ Being blamed for things that are not our fault.
⇨ Physical punishment.
⇨ Being told we are 'useless' or will 'never amount to anything'.
⇨ Being told we are responsible for other people's unhappiness.
⇨ Being ridiculed/humiliated.
⇨ Being bullied.
⇨ Experience of sexual abuse.

If we are fortunate and have basically favourable conditions and experiences whilst we are growing up, we are likely to develop healthy self-esteem and be confident people. However, if conditions and experiences are mainly negative, we are more likely to experience difficulties liking ourselves and being confident; some of the negative messages we have received will have been accepted by us and become part of what we think and feel about ourselves.

Recent and current experiences

Recent and current experiences then affect our self-esteem and confidence. We often interpret them in order to fit in with our view of ourselves. A person lacking in self-esteem who receives a low mark for an assignment may think, 'What else could I expect? I'm stupid, this proves it, I might as well leave.' A person with healthy self-esteem who receives a low mark may think, 'I wonder where I went wrong? I'll find out so that I can

do better next time.' Although this person may feel disappointed, s/he does not feel diminished as a person by the low mark.

If we have little self-esteem then the 'low mark' scenario may trigger memories of similar events in the past and then lead to negative thinking in the form of self-critical put-downs. This is how we intensify and perpetuate low self-esteem and lack confidence. When we feel low like this, our expectations about the future tend to be negative and this discourages us from really trying. Then we experience another disappointing result and feel negative about ourselves again.

Improving self-esteem and confidence

Practising self-acceptance
We can improve our self-esteem and confidence in a number of ways. One of the most important ways of increasing our self-esteem is to become more accepting of ourselves. We can develop an attitude of self-acceptance such that we feel okay about ourselves whilst recognising that we are imperfect and capable of making mistakes.

We can start by noticing situations which influence our self-esteem, particularly those which diminish it. By consistently taking notice of our fluctuating levels of self-esteem we may discover important information about ourselves. Perhaps we only feel good about ourselves when:
⇨ We are successful.
⇨ We are putting other people first.
⇨ When we are in a relationship.
⇨ When we are making money.

Perhaps we feel bad about ourselves when:
⇨ We end a relationship.
⇨ We say 'No' to someone.
⇨ We disagree with other people.

We need to practice self-acceptance, feeling okay about ourselves, regardless of any conditions. If we make mistakes, hurt or offend other people, it may be appropriate to make amends, but it need not lead to self-dislike. In this way, we may sometimes think it is reasonable to be critical of our behaviour and try to change it, but without being critical of ourselves. We can therefore recognise our faults without beating ourselves up over them. This attitude helps maintain a healthy level of self-esteem by:

⇨ Making a distinction between who we are and what we do.
⇨ Recognising that we need not be perfect before we start liking ourselves.

Recognising good qualities and abilities

We can boost our self-esteem and confidence by recognising our good qualities and abilities. Regularly reminding ourselves of them can be helpful. If it doesn't come easily, then we can start with the experience of being a student; we must be good at several things and possess a number of skills to have come this far. The same applies if we have a job or have ever had a job; we have skills/qualities which others appreciate. We can ask a friend what s/he likes about us; this can help us recognise qualities we may have overlooked.

Seeking out positive experiences and people

We can give ourselves positive experiences as a way of increasing our self-esteem and confidence. Also, spending time with people who like us for who we are is helpful. Being around negative and critical people most of the time or withdrawing from social contact can have a detrimental effect on how we feel about ourselves.

Hints for making changes

If, as a result of monitoring our self-esteem and confidence, we decide that we want to change, it is best to identify some specific goals. Having done that, it is necessary to make sure that they are manageable; break it down into smaller steps or identify a less ambitious change to attempt first. For example, in order to be able to speak up in seminars, it may be easier to begin by expressing opinions more often with friends. Becoming comfortable with this can make the next step, contributing in a seminar, easier.

Positive rehearsal

This technique can help build up confidence for tackling a situation which may seem daunting. It is most effective if practised several times before attempting the real thing. It takes about 15 minutes of uninterrupted time.

⇨ Find a comfortable position, either lying down or on a chair which offers good support.
⇨ Focus on your breathing.
⇨ Make the 'out' breath longer than the 'in' breath.

⇨ In your head, say the word 'Peace' or 'Calm' on the 'in' breath.
⇨ Continue breathing steadily like this and enjoy the feeling of relaxation as it spreads over you.
⇨ When feeling comfortably relaxed, begin to imagine your chosen situation.
⇨ Make it as detailed and as vivid as you can.
⇨ Imagine handling it in the best possible way and with a favourable outcome.
⇨ Upon reaching the end of this rehearsal, continue breathing calmly to allow yourself time to 'come to' slowly.

Rewards and support

Give yourself rewards as you practice building your self-esteem. It doesn't really matter what the reward is, as long as it is something you value. It may be a night out, a bar of chocolate, eating your favourite food or watching your favourite TV programme or film.

If you can, tell a good friend what you are doing; their encouragement and feedback on the changes you are making could be invaluable.

⇨ The above information is reprinted with kind permission from the University of Wolverhampton. Visit www.wlv.ac.uk for more.

© University of Wolverhampton

Building your child's confidence and self-esteem

Information from the Family Matters Institute

From the time a child is born and right through their life span, he or she is constantly developing mentally, socially and physically. Society has a great responsibility in areas of a child's development like their confidence and self-esteem. The more positive children feel about themselves, the greater their self-esteem and the better adjusted they are.

Self-esteem or self-image refers to the perception that people have of themselves. Children base their

Family Matters Institute

self-esteem on the opinions they feel other people have of them. A child who gets positive vibes from his/her parents and other people in society will grow up feeling loved, cared

for and have a high self-esteem. On the other hand, children who are constantly subjected to criticism, made to feel that they can never do anything right, not appreciated and excluded will end up with a very low self-esteem.

Children do not acquire self-esteem automatically. Self-esteem is built over a period of time. A child may feel good about themselves at home, but not quite have such a positive self-image in the company of his/her friends or at school. It is important for parents to realise that a child needs to feel that they are special and are appreciated. It is good when a parent can make a child realise that regardless of what happens outside the home, within the home environment they have the full support of their parents.

There are a few conditions which ensure that self-esteem remains high – remember the word 'IMAGE'.

Included

Your child needs to feel included at home, in the community or in school. As a parent, you can ensure that at least at home he/she feels a sense of belonging and is included and an integral part of the home life.

Mirror

Whatever you think of your child and the way you interact with him/her will be mirrored in his/her behaviour and self-esteem. So, if you are constantly negative with him/her, his/her self-esteem will mirror this and he/she will have a low opinion of himself.

Appreciation

Words like 'thank you' and 'well done' go a long way in rebuilding someone's broken self-image and their lack of self-worth. It shows that you as a parent care and appreciate what your child has done.

Good feelings

Make your child feel good about themselves with praise and love.

Encouragement

Your child may not be confident about doing something. Encourage them to go ahead and make them feel supported.

Parents play an extremely important role in a child's development. Taking your child seriously, appreciating them and giving them love and encouragement will help develop their character and personality, so that they grow up to be balanced and confident individuals with a high sense of self-esteem.

Be positive and loving.

⇨ The above information is reprinted with kind permission from the Family Matters Institute. Visit www.familymatters.org.uk for more information.

© FMI

Assertiveness

Information from TheSite

Constantly feel like a doormat? Do your superiors make unreasonable demands that you just can't say 'no' to? Then it's time to get assertive.

What is it?

Assertiveness is a way of expressing your thoughts, feelings and beliefs in a direct, honest and appropriate way.

An assertive person effectively influences, listens and negotiates so that others choose to cooperate willingly. It does not mean being aggressive, nor does it mean you will get your own way all the time. But it should help prevent you being burdened with other people's problems and responsibilities.

Assert yourself

If you tend to panic, hide under your desk or fly off the handle at the first whiff of a problem, you probably need to take heed of these tips and assert yourself in the office.

Be clear about what you want to say

Make direct statements that take responsibility for what you say, i.e. use 'I' rather than 's/he' or 'everyone thinks'.

Get straight to the point

Don't allow yourself to get side-tracked by colleagues or by trying to soften the blow.

Be prepared to compromise

Remember that other people have rights too; don't become the office bully.

Use suitable facial expressions

Maintain good eye contact and keep your voice firm but pleasant. By keeping calm and attentive you will make the other person more ready to compromise.

Listen

Let people know you have heard what they said. This doesn't mean you have to agree with them.

Ask for time to think, if necessary

There is nothing wrong with admitting that you need time to make a decision.

Don't apologise unless there is a good reason to do so

Don't say 'sorry' merely because the other person is unlikely to be pleased with what you are saying. It is better to give reasons rather than excuses for what you want to do.

Learn to say no to unreasonable requests

Use the word 'no' and offer an explanation if you choose to. Do not apologise and do not make up excuses. Paraphrase the other person's point of view. This will let him/her know that you hear and understand the request.

Often you can get assertiveness training within the workplace or at a local evening class. Ask your boss or contact your local careers centre for more information.

⇨ The above information is reprinted with kind permission from TheSite. Visit www.thesite.org for more information for young adults aged 16-25.

© TheSite.org

How do other people see you?

Until you accept who you are, you won't be revealing your true self to the world, says Emma Cook

You're walking down the street and, quite unexpectedly, you catch sight of yourself, on CCTV, in a shop window. You're confronted with a 'real' version of yourself, one that's indefinably different to the snapshot you carry in your head. Is that really what I look like? The discord between self-image and how the world views you is ruthlessly exposed. When it comes to personality, however, there is no camera to physically reflect back that chasm between the internal and external. Instead, you must rely on your own powers of self-awareness or other people's honesty – neither particularly reliable or objective measures.

Accept yourself

Many of us labour under the belief that we are less attractive, successful or amusing than the people we know, and have no idea how others perceive us. It often comes as a surprise when we learn other people are impressed by us, or, conversely, that they think we're lazy or rude. Most of the time we are unaware of the gap between how others see us and how we see ourselves – but we could learn a lot from being conscious of how we come across to others.

According to psychologists, the more aware and accepting you are of your strengths and weaknesses, the more honest and open you can be with others. When people know you for who you really are, and feel comfortable in your presence, this reaffirms your sense of self-confidence, empathy and awareness. Psychologists refer to such an ideal state of synchronicity between what you know about yourself, what you reveal to the world and what comes back to you, as 'congruence'.

'It's about having enough self-knowledge to know how and why you behave a certain way in certain situations, and to then have the confidence to communicate that knowledge,' explains life coach Fiona Reed. Reed admits that she herself can be rather bossy in certain situations, but is quite open about it. 'I know if I'm upfront about it, it saves people saying, "Oh, she's really bossy." It takes away the power of gossip from other people.'

Many of us labour under the belief that we are less attractive, successful or amusing than the people we know

---

One of her key values in life is congruence; being true to herself in any given situation. 'Those that are able to express their real self are much more likely to be popular,' she says. 'People want to be around you when you're comfortable with yourself. It also means there's a fluency in how you fit in with the world; you're not trying to hide anything, consciously or unconsciously.'

It is this instinct to conceal elements of your self – in most cases the parts we find most unpalatable – that creates disparity between self-perception and how others see us. To some extent, we all do it because we're driven by the same desire; to be liked, to do well in the eyes of others, and to feel popular and loved.

Rosa, 31, a marketing manager, is constantly frustrated by Alison, a trainee. 'She's desperate to please the whole time, which has the effect of making people dislike her. She tries to second-guess your opinion rather than admitting what she really thinks about anything. I never know her views. Often I just want to shake her and say, "Come on, what's your opinion?"'

Fence-sitting is a classic people-pleasing tactic; Alison will assume that because she agrees with her manager, she won't provoke her and she's more likely to win her affection. Yet this desperation to shape external perception only creates a negative impression. People such as this are more likely to experience 'imposter syndrome', the fear of being discovered as a fraud. It's all wrapped up in low self-esteem: the sense that, 'If you find out about me, you won't like me at all.'

People-pleasers are also much more likely to underestimate how well others view them; part of the problem is they assume everyone judges by their own impossibly high standards. 'I'm always amazed if I find out someone has said they think I'm intelligent,' says Katy, 45, a financial manager and Cambridge graduate. 'It just doesn't ring true; I always see myself as only an A-minus.' (In her eyes, a low score.) At the other extreme, there are those who consistently overestimate what others think of them. In terms of congruence, the over-estimators are surprisingly similar to the under-estimators; it is low self-esteem expressed in a different way.

Warped self-perception

Our ability to recognise and accept who we are is, inevitably, influenced by upbringing. 'If you can't or won't recognise who you are, you're more likely to have had an unhappy or emotionally-deprived childhood,' says psychologist Clare Wilson. 'You'll also be starting out with a filter through which you'll only see things that you want to see.'

The major obstacle that stops most of us tackling this 'filter' between how others view us and how we view ourselves is fear. 'People play roles because they're scared they're not good enough,' says Wilson. 'They're hoping to build themselves up in some way, to hide what they feel is unacceptable about themselves.'

It can also be damaging for anyone on the receiving end. Becky, 35, used to work with a woman who was widely known in the office to be a bully. 'She would get hysterical and start screaming at me, making me feel terrible. Yet one friend knew my boss socially and would tell me how sweet she was outside work – and that she'd be devastated if she knew how she came across.' However badly she behaved, this woman could only view herself as someone people were always trying to push around.

The only way to clear such warped self-perceptions is to get a glimpse of ourselves from the outside. 'I often record my sessions with clients,' says Professor Stephen Palmer, director of the coaching psychology unit at City University. 'It's quite a shock to them to listen to themselves in conversation – people can get very good insights into how others see them.'

Which is why 360-degree evaluations – feedback from other staff members about how you come across – are increasingly popular, although rather terrifying.

'You have to be prepared to be exposed,' says Reed. 'Ask friends what they think of you. Therapy and coaching can only take you so far – hearing it directly from those around you is the best way to get a realistic insight.'

Of course, how you absorb this is also key to viewing yourself in realistic terms. It's no good if you dismiss

external perceptions on the one hand or take it too much to heart and feel crushed on the other. 'You can't take on what others are saying about you if you're defensive,' says Wilson.

It's also helpful to remember that others' perception of you is also subjective. 'Don't assume others see us accurately,' says Wilson. 'Everyone has their own filters through which they see the world, which will affect how they see you.' This is why trying to second-guess others' impressions – and caring desperately what they're thinking in the first place - is so unrewarding. Much better to question and analyse your own needs, and to reflect on how your actions may affect those around you.

You'll know you've moved on when the thought of external feedback – from friends, family or colleagues – no longer makes you feel insecure and anxious.

Are you creating a perception gap?

If you answer 'yes' to any of the following questions, your inner 'you' doesn't match the 'you' that others see.

⇨ Do you care what others think about you? Are you paranoid you've created the wrong impression, obsessing about trivial details in conversations? You may underestimate how well others think of you.

⇨ Do you feel exhausted after a day at work and short-tempered at home once you can let your guard down? This is a sign of people-pleasing; the effort of presenting a different 'you' is so tiring that, when you're behind closed doors, the anger

and resentment spills out.

⇨ Do you tidy up your house scrupulously before anyone comes round? This is a good way of judging how much you care what others think of you. How much do you care if people see your mess?

⇨ If someone says something negative about you, how much does it hurt? If you're secure, congruent and know who you are, says psychologist Clare Wilson, a criticism won't be wounding. You're more likely to feel, 'This is part of being me. If I can accept it, I hope others can, too.'

Close the perception gap
Mirroring technique
In this exercise, get a friend to relate her feelings on a subject you don't agree with and then repeat back, after each sentence, what she has said. Think about exactly what she's saying and why, after you repeat her words. 'This is a good way of stepping into someone else's shoes and building empathy,' says psychologist Honey Langcaster-James.
Self-reflection
You have to reflect on your own behaviour, and consider how other people react to you and why, says Professor Stephen Palmer. Think about what you project onto others. Be prepared to be exposed, says life coach Fiona Reed. Ask close friends and loved ones what they really think about the messages you're giving out.

⇨ The above information is reprinted with kind permission from Psychologies. Visit www.psychologies. co.uk for more information.
© Psychologies

High self-esteem not always what it's cracked up to be

Study warns of high self-esteem that is fragile and shallow. By Philip Lee Williams

Oscar Levant, a mid-century pianist, film star and wit, once watched noted keyboardist and composer George Gershwin spend an evening playing his own music at a party and clearly having a great time.

'Tell me, George,' Levant said, somewhat jealously, 'if you have it to do all over again would you still fall in love with yourself?'

Increasingly, psychologists are looking at such behaviour and saying out loud what may go against the grain of how many people act: high self-esteem is not the same thing as healthy self-esteem. And new research by a psychology professor from the University of Georgia is adding another twist: those with 'secure' high self-esteem are less likely to be verbally defensive than those who have 'fragile' high self-esteem.

'There are many kinds of high self-esteem, and in this study we found that for those in which it is fragile and shallow it's no better than having low self-esteem,' said Michael Kernis. 'People with fragile high self-esteem compensate for their self-doubts by engaging in exaggerated tendencies to defend, protect and enhance their feelings of self-worth.'

The research was published today in the Journal of Personality. Kernis's co-authors are Chad Lakey and Whitney Heppner, both doctoral students in the UGA social psychology program.

Amid the complexity of perspectives on the human psyche, a slow but relentless change is occurring in how psychologists view self-esteem, said Kernis. It was once thought that more self-esteem necessarily is better self-esteem. In recent years, however, high self-esteem per se has come under attack on several fronts, especially in areas such as aggressive behaviour. Also, individuals with high self-esteem sometimes become very unlikable when others or events threaten their egos.

While high self-esteem is still generally valued as a good quality that is important to a happy and productive life, more researchers are breaking it down into finer gradations and starting to understand when high self-esteem turns from good to bad. In fact, it is now thought that there are multiple forms of high self-esteem, only some of which consistently relate to positive psychological functioning.

One of the ways in which high self-esteem can turn bad is when it is accompanied by verbal defensiveness – lashing out at others when a person's opinions, beliefs, statements or values are threatened. So Kernis and his colleagues designed a study, reported in the current article, to see if respondents whose self-esteem is 'fragile' were more verbally defensive than those whose self-esteem was 'secure.'

Using 100 undergraduates, they set up a study in three phases. In the first part, students completed a basic demographic questionnaire and other measures to evaluate their levels and other aspects of self-esteem. In phase two, the team assessed the students' stability of self-esteem because the more unstable or variable one's self-esteem, the more fragile it is. And finally, in the last phase, the researchers conducted a structured 'life experiences interview' to measure what they call 'defensive verbalisation'.

'Our findings offer strong support for a multi-component model of self-esteem that highlights the distinction between its fragile and secure forms,' said Kernis. 'Individuals with low self-esteem or fragile high self-esteem were more verbally defensive than individuals with secure high self-esteem. One reason for this is that potential threats are in fact more threatening to people with low or fragile high self-esteem than those with secure high self-esteem, and so they work harder to counteract them.'

On the other hand, individuals with secure high self-esteem appear to accept themselves 'warts and all,' and, feeling less threatened, they are less likely to be defensive by blaming others or providing excuses when they speak about past transgressions or threatening experiences.

One reason the study's findings are important, Kernis said, is that it shows that greater verbal defensiveness relates to lower psychological well-being and life satisfaction.

'These findings support the view that heightened defensiveness reflects insecurity, fragility and less-than-optimal functioning rather than a healthy psychological outlook,' said Kernis. 'We aren't suggesting there's something wrong with people when they want to feel good about themselves. What we are saying is that when feeling good about themselves becomes a prime directive, for these people excessive defensiveness and self-promotion are likely to follow, the self-esteem is likely to be fragile rather than secure and any psychological benefits will be very limited.'

And what of Oscar Levant and George Gershwin? While Levant now may be largely remembered for his acid opinions, Gershwin left us *Rhapsody in Blue*, *An American in Paris*, and *Porgy and Bess*, three of the most memorable compositions of the 20th century.

So the score for that fabled encounter on the secure self-esteem scale could be Gershwin 1, Levant, 0. Maybe it's a reminder of the complicated nature of self-esteem. *28 April 2008*

Can we teach people to be happy?

Anthony Seldon and Frank Furedi set out their arguments before the first of a series of live public debates on educational issues

Yes, says Anthony Seldon

There is only one important question: what is the purpose of education? Is it to cram students with facts to maximise their test performances, so that whole institutions become exam factories, tensing and stretching every sinew to achieve five A*s-Cs at GCSE, and comparable results at A-level and beyond?

Or is there a wider vision? One that involves developing the whole student, so that we help them know who they are and what they want to do in life. On leaving full-time education, not only will they be able to wave certificates with pass marks written on them, they will also be fully prepared to embrace life in all its fullness.

Schooling at present is driven by three forces: the government, universities and employers.

The government wants to show, year on year, a quantifiable improvement in results that will show it is 'doing a good job for education'. It has little incentive to concern itself with holistic and non-measurable aspects of learning.

Universities want to have the brightest possible pupils in their departments. Some take into account wider achievement. But, overwhelmingly, universities are concerned with GCSE and A-level results. This does not encourage schools or pupils to want to broaden out.

As for employers, I am not certain I understand what they want.

These three 'top-down' drivers all have their place, but they are far too dominant. Children need to achieve results academically, not least to maximise their employment prospects. But this should be balanced with 'bottom-up' factors: what makes up each child, and how can they make the most of their linguistic and logical, social and personal, spiritual and moral, creative and physical faculties? Every school should be developing these eight aptitudes. And the less privileged the children, the greater the role of the school. What isn't developed when young may never be.

Most important of all is the relationship with oneself

Why should we teach children how to live and how to be happy? Three reasons. First, if schools do not, children may never learn elsewhere. Second, depression, self-harming and anxiety among students are reaching epidemic proportions. So are drinking and drug-taking. Teaching schoolchildren how to live autonomous lives increases the chances of avoiding depression, mental illness and dependency when they are older.

And third, since the development of the positive psychology movement under Martin Seligman and developments in neuroscience, we now know how to teach wellbeing, and have empirical evidence of its effectiveness. But what should one teach?

The emphasis is on relationships. In ascending order of importance, the relationship with technology comes first. Young people can spend 30 hours a week in front of television and computers screens. In wellbeing classes, they learn how to use technology rather than to be used by it.

Then, they learn how to relate to the environment around them, including how to organise their rooms and possessions to give them a sense of order.

Relating to others is fundamental because nothing is a greater source of joy, nor of anguish, than human relationships. Students learn how to foster friendships that nourish them and avoid those which are destructive. Good relationships are crucial not only in families but also in the workplace.

Most important of all is the relationship with oneself. Students learn how to manage their minds, their emotions and their bodies. Bit by bit, they learn what makes them distinctive.

They learn to recognise and manage their negative and positive emotions. They learn the value of accepting themselves as they are and appreciating others. They are taught to calm themselves by deep breathing and other techniques, and discover that three 20-minute bouts of exercise a week have the same effect on raising the spirit and avoiding depression as a standard dose of Prozac.

In Britain today, we have exam instruction, rather than the education of the whole person. This is as unnecessary as it is unkind. We need educational environments that develop all the intelligences of every student.

Anthony Seldon is master of Wellington College.

No, says Frank Furedi

In recent years, officials and educational experts have sought to solve the problems afflicting learning environments through behaviour management. Increasingly, the focus is on students' 'wellbeing', 'emotional literacy' and 'self-esteem'. Since this reorientation, the ambitions of therapeutic education have gone from strength to strength. Yet there is no evidence that it works.

In schools, decades of silly programmes designed to raise children's self-esteem have not improved wellbeing

It is depressing news that the self-help manual has made it on to the university curriculum. In therapy-obsessed America, positive psychology is one of the most popular new classes at Harvard. And Britain is going the same way, with a whole institute devoted to wellbeing at Cambridge.

In schools, decades of silly programmes designed to raise children's self-esteem have not improved wellbeing, and the new initiatives designed to make pupils happy will also fail. Worse still, emotional education encourages an inward-looking orientation that distracts children from engaging with the world.

Perversely, the ascendancy of psychobabble in the classroom has been paralleled by an apparent increase in mental health problems among children. The relationship between the two is not accidental. Children are highly suggestible, and the more they are required to participate in wellbeing classes, the more they will feel the need for professional support.

The teaching of emotional literacy and happiness should be viewed as a displacement activity by professionals who find it difficult to confront the many challenges they face. At a time when many schools find it difficult to engage children's interest in core subjects, and to inspire a culture of high aspiration, it is tempting to look for non-academic solutions. Many pedagogues find it easier to hold forth about making children feel good about themselves than to teach them how to read and count. This therapeutic orientation serves to distract pupils and teachers alike from getting on with the job of gaining a real education.

Educators have always hoped that their work would inspire their students, and make them feel good about learning and life. But, until recently, happiness was not seen as an end in itself or something to be promoted on its own terms.

Everyday experience suggests that not everything that has to be learned can be taught. How to feel well is not a suitable subject for teaching. Why? Because genuine happiness is experienced through the interaction of the individual with the challenges thrown up by life. One reason why well-meaning educators cannot teach their pupils to be happy is because feelings are contingent on encounters and relationships.

As Franklin D. Roosevelt said, happiness 'lies in the joy of achievement, in the thrill of creative effort'. Students can learn about their emotions, develop a sense of self and, occasionally, experience happiness through engaging with literature, art and other intellectual challenges, but not by being instructed on how to feel, or how to manage emotions.

Once it becomes part of the curriculum, happiness ceases to be an emotional response to our experiences. It is turned into a formula that can be taught by teachers, learned by students and managed by policy-makers. Being happy becomes associated with a skill whose acquisition can be measured and turned into a government target. This approach to emotional life will distract educators from dealing intelligently with the existential problems confronting their learners. Students need to understand the moral meaning of good before they can feel 'good' about themselves.

Experience suggests that the very idea that we should all aspire to happiness is insipid. People experience a range of emotions – including sadness – when confronted with poignant tales from history, and tragic stories from literature. In our vapid emotional era, it is worth recalling that a good life is not always a happy one. People are often justified in being unhappy about their circumstances and surroundings. Discontent and ambition have driven humanity to confront and overcome the challenges they face. That is why characters such as the Controller in *Brave New World* want us to live on a diet of 'feelies' and 'scent organs'. That is also why we should be suspicious of experts who seek to colonise our internal life.

Frank Furedi is a professor of sociology at the University of Kent.
19 February 2008

Psychologists research the rollercoaster of life

Information from the British Psychological Society

Everyone has their ups and downs, but psychologists presenting their research at the British Psychological Society Developmental Section Conference at Oxford Brookes University, held on the 2 September 2008, have discovered that for many of us, the highs and lows of the roller-coaster of life may run along very similar tracks.

Children aged eight and nine had high levels of self-esteem and optimism, but this dipped in adolescence

---

Psychologists from the Open University surveyed more than 16,000 people aged from 8 to 85 to look for patterns in psychological wellbeing across the human life span and the sexes.

Participants filled out online questionnaires measuring their self-esteem, optimism and whether they felt life was in their own control, or the control of external forces. These factors are all known to be important dimensions of psychological functioning.

Professor David Messer said: 'We found some really interesting patterns across our sample. When we looked at measures of self-esteem we found that children aged eight and nine had high levels of self-esteem and optimism, but this dipped in adolescence. 16- and 17-year-olds had the lowest levels of self-esteem and 14- to 21-year-olds the lowest levels of optimism. Levels of self-esteem and optimism climbed back up, reaching a peak in the late thirties. The 34- to 39-year-old age group in our study had the highest levels. Self-esteem dipped again after 50, especially in men, although over the entire lifespan men had significantly higher self-esteem than women.'

The researchers also looked at who people felt was in the driving seat across their life span, and found that feelings of control also shifted across the different age groups. In this sample they saw that children had high levels of external control, reflecting the control of their parents. Into adulthood, respondents felt in control of their own lives – they had high levels of internal control. However, in later adulthood feelings then shifted back to external control with the 50- to 53-year-old age group having the highest levels of external control across the whole sample. They also found that women more than men felt that their lives were dictated by external factors.

Over the entire life span men had significantly higher self-esteem than women

---

John Oates, co-author of the study, said: 'The patterns of self esteem, optimism and feelings of control from childhood through to old age that emerged from our research are really interesting. Many of these patterns can be explained by changes in education, career building, family and social life and cultural values that most of us in this country experience.

'Although of course individuals have their ups and downs due to personal circumstances, these highs and lows of our psychological wellbeing may actually be fairly consistent and predictable. You could say that although we are all in our own seats and experiencing different rides, we're all on the same rollercoaster.'

This data was collected from a predominantly British sample of people who had accessed web pages related to the popular BBC television documentary *Child of Our Time*.
2 September 2008

⇨ The above information is reprinted with kind permission from the British Psychological Society. Visit www.bps.org.uk for more information.
© *British Psychological Society*

Teens and body image

Tips on liking the skin that you're in

What is body image, and why is it such a difficult issue for teens? Learn what body image is, signs of body image problems, and how to improve your body image.

What is body image?

Body image has to do with how you think about your size and shape. How you think about your body relates to how you think about yourself as a whole, so a negative body image is often linked to low self-esteem, anxiety, depression and feeling bad about yourself. Many people with a negative body image struggle with eating disorders, dieting and self-doubt.

Why is it important to have a positive body image?

A healthy body image is essential to your health, happiness and well-being. People with a healthy body image are less likely to engage in self-destructive habits such as crash dieting, smoking to lose weight, excessive drinking, self-harming, and bingeing and purging. They are more likely to feel good about themselves overall and see the way they look as one small part of who they are and less likely to beat themselves up when they have too many french fries or a big slice of cake.

Why do so many teens struggle with a negative body image?

For some, a negative body image is made worse by comparing themselves to models and actors on TV, in the movies and in magazines, even though the body type many of them represent is not realistic or healthy for most people.

Teens in particular tend to struggle with body image because they're self-conscious about the changes their bodies are going through during puberty. As your body grows and develops, some parts fill out more

quickly than others. Genes play a big role, too: some people inherit a very fast metabolism or a very lean body type, while a more muscular build runs in other families. Unfortunately, our culture tends to glorify some body types and discount others, rather than focusing on what's healthy and realistic.

What are the signs of an unhealthy body image?

A lot of the signs of an unhealthy body image are internal: negative or obsessive thoughts about food, self-hatred, constantly comparing oneself to others, etc. Some people constantly think about getting breast implants or having liposuction.

Some people with a negative body image will weigh themselves multiple times a day, obsessively exercise or count calories, or diet constantly. Some people cut or burn themselves to deal with the shame they feel about their bodies. Others force themselves to throw up (purging) or stop eating altogether. These are symptoms of a more serious eating disorder. Still others abuse drugs such as heroin or steroids to achieve the body type that

they want – while putting their health in great danger.

How can I improve my body image?

Improving your body image takes time, and it also involves improving your self-esteem in most cases. The first step involves accepting your body, no matter how big, small, fat, thin, dark or light it is. When you have a negative thought about your body, tell yourself to stop and remind yourself of something that you like about yourself or the way you look.

It's also important to recognise that there are some things about yourself that you can't change – and that, for the most part, don't matter that much. So you've got chubby fingers or big feet, who really cares? Most people don't notice, and if they do, it probably doesn't matter to them nearly as much as it matters to you. What you're like – not what you look like – is what counts.

⇨ The above information is reprinted with kind permission from about. com. Visit www.teenadvice.about. com for more information.

© About.com

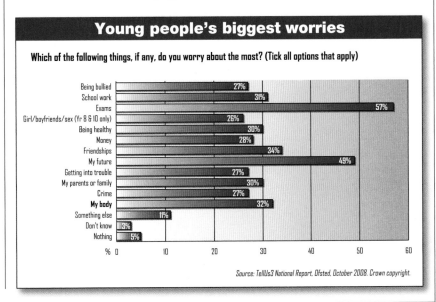

Young people's biggest worries

Which of the following things, if any, do you worry about the most? (Tick all options that apply)

	%
Being bullied	27%
School work	31%
Exams	57%
Girl/boyfriends/sex (Yr 8 & 10 only)	26%
Being healthy	30%
Money	28%
Friendships	34%
My future	49%
Getting into trouble	27%
My parents or family	30%
Crime	27%
My body	32%
Something else	11%
Don't know	3%
Nothing	5%

Source: TellUs3 National Report, Ofsted, October 2008. Crown copyright.

Mirror image

How do you feel about your reflection?

Feel too fat? Scared you're too skinny? Fed up with your thighs? Embarrassed by your bum? You'd be hard pushed to find anybody who didn't tick at least one of these boxes.

Teens First for Health has been swamped with emails from weight worriers. If you're not concerned about being too fat, then you hate how skinny you are. If you aren't seeking the secret to bigger boobs, you're asking how to make them smaller. No matter what size or shape you are, none of you seem happy with your bodies.

Bliss magazine asked 2000 girls, aged between 10 and 19, how they felt about their bodies. A whopping nine out of ten confessed they weren't happy with how they looked:

⇨ Two-thirds thought they needed to lose weight.

⇨ 64 per cent of girls under 13 had been on a diet.

⇨ Over a quarter of 14-year-olds had considered plastic surgery.

Big deal, some of you might say – the scary thing is that it can be a pretty big deal. We all have bad hair days now and then but, for more and more people, these insecurities are becoming real problems. Low self-esteem can be a trigger for anorexia, bulimia and binge-eating, and it can be the reason why overweight people don't have the confidence to change their lifestyle.

Food for thought

When we feel truly happy, how we look doesn't seem to matter quite so much. Ask yourself if there's other emotional niggles and worries you need to put right first.

'People should only get judged by who they are. Originality, uniqueness and character are what count. Be yourself and you'll go far.'
Sam and Charlotte, 16, beat ambassadors

Slim-crazy society

Everyday the media bulldozes us with shock stories and bad diet warnings. Jamie Oliver declares war on school dinners, while Gillian McKeith dissects poo, and obesity rates hit the headlines, warning us to change our ways or suffer the consequences. On the other hand, there's the size zero debate, with models being banned for being too skinny. Weekly glossies plaster their pages with cruel cellulite-spotting pap shots one week, and then expose celebs' emaciated bodies the next. It's all pretty confusing, which is why it's no wonder many of us have a distorted view of our bodies.

'One way to develop and maintain a positive self-image is to remember that how you look isn't the only thing people care about, or what makes you you. Think about what you value in others to work out what other qualities and skills are important to you.'
Katy Phillips, psychologist, Great Ormond Street Hospital

Beauty is in its imperfections

The secret to looking and feeling good doesn't come in the shape of a syringe or a crash diet plan; it's about learning to love yourself. It may sound cheesy, but imagine how much more fun life would be if we weren't burdened with body-conscious hang-ups.

Katy Phillips, a psychologist at Great Ormond Street, offers some confidence-boosting tricks:

⇨ Ask yourself (and people you trust) whether the things you hate about your body really are flaws. Do you have unrealistic expectations of yourself? If you expect yourself to look perfect in all situations, all of the time, then you are setting yourself up to fail. Factors such as illness, tiredness, periods and so on mean that being perfect all day, everyday is impossible to achieve. Even supposedly flawless celebrities will have bad days.

⇨ Are you forgetting to notice positive things about yourself? Some people only notice photos of themselves they hate and will ignore any compliments people pay them.

⇨ Are you discounting positive information that you do notice? Many people will react to a compliment by thinking that the person must be lying.

⇨ Learn to be kind to yourself. Ask yourself whether it would be fair for you to be as critical to a friend. If not, then maybe it is not fair to you either. Try to develop a caring and forgiving approach to yourself, just as you might do with others.

Take a break

Another classic culprit for knocking confidence is comparing yourself to other people, especially models, TV or film stars. Remember the images you see aren't really real – they've been airbrushed to perfection, and the celebs

have been nipped, tucked, covered in concealer and preened in preparation. This is their day job and they spend hours working at 'appearing' perfect.

What we can learn from A-list lovelies is that exuding confidence draws people to you. You won't see many down-in-the-dumps divas being snapped on the red carpet or selling products on the pages of glossy mags. People naturally like people who like themselves, so try to banish your blues with a smile and stop stressing over your appearance.

Weight issues

Your weight, like your height and looks, depends a lot on your genes, your build and your diet. If you're worried you might be overweight, you could check this out on a table showing normal height and weight. Ask your school nurse or doctor for advice – there are special tables designed for

young people, which are different to those for adults aged 20 and over.

'It's normal to have some body image concerns because adjusting to bodily changes during puberty involves considering whether these changes feel ok,' says Katy Phillips. 'And this can take a bit of time.'

'Try not to compare yourself to your friends. Remember that everyone develops at a different time in a different way, so making comparisons usually leads to unnecessary anxiety.'
Katy Phillips, psychologist

Exercise down-in-the-dump demons

⇨ Write down all your good points (don't hold back!). Pin this list above the mirror in your room, read it regularly and update it. Imagine someone else has all these traits – would this person be your

friend? Would you like them?
⇨ Get outdoors and shake off that sluggishness. You've heard it all before, but only because it's true! Exercise releases feel-good chemicals and keeps you healthy.
⇨ Before you go to sleep think of five things that made you happy that day – no matter how tiny (a special text) or big (acing an exam).
⇨ Clear up clutter: tidy your bedroom, get rid of old clothes, add some sunshine to your bedroom and do it all with your favourite music in the background.
25 February 2008

⇨ This article has been reproduced with kind permission from Children First for Health – Great Ormond Street Hospital's leading health information website for young people of all ages and parents: www.childrenfirst.nhs.uk.

© *Great Ormond Street Hospital*

Problems and improvement

Information from My Body Beautiful

Instead of embarking on a more meaningful quest women have placed their faith in products and images. Rather than loving their bodies, and being peaceful, respectful, and gentle with them, women have attacked, manipulated, and controlled their physical selves, never feeling satisfied or content.' (*'Body Wars'*, p. 10)

A person's body image is their perception of their physical appearance. It is more than what a person thinks about what they see in a mirror, but is inextricably tied to their self-esteem. A person with a poor body image will perceive their own body as being unattractive or even repulsive to others, while a person with good body image, or positive 'body acceptance', will either see themselves as attractive to others, or will at least accept their body as it is. Body image is most strongly affected during puberty, and is influenced by peers, parents, teachers, mentors and commercial advertising.

1. The trouble with body image
Mind and emotions
Individuals with a poor body image tend to be preoccupied with aspects of their physical appearance. The more dissatisfied they are with the way they look, particularly if they consistently compare themselves unfavourably to others, the greater the adverse effects on their mind and emotions will be.
Actions
A person with a poor body image will often alter their actions to avoid situations that make them uncomfortable. This may take the form of wearing baggy unfashionable clothes, avoiding social activities and shying away from close romantic relationships.
Self-esteem
Self-esteem (self-worth) is often a measurement of how a person feels about their body. If someone is engrossed in thoughts of their physical appearance, they often overlook the fact that they are a valuable, loveable, unique human being, packed with natural gifts, skills and abilities... much more than just a body.

Tunnel vision
Individuals who are obsessed with the need to change their appearance tend to spend so much time focussed on this aspect of themselves that they can fail to cultivate and develop other ambitions and skills. This will result in further failures, e.g. unfulfilled dreams in other areas of their life.
Depression
Prolonged unhappiness with one's appearance can develop into depression. Depression is a mental state characterised by feelings of sadness, despair and discouragement. There are often feelings of low self-esteem, guilt, self reproach, social withdrawal and physical symptoms such as eating and sleep disturbances.
Eating disorders
Eating disorders are a group of mental disorders that interfere with normal food consumption. They may lead to serious health problems and, in the case of both Bulimia Nervosa and Anorexia Nervosa, even death. Individuals suffering from an eating disorder often have a distorted body image.

2. Negative body image

Seeking perfection

Today, women, and a growing number of men, are focused on doing whatever it takes to achieve the perfect body. The problem with this is that the culturally defined 'perfect body' can only be achieved by a very small number of the population, i.e. those born with the required genetic make-up. Thus for the vast majority of us the ideal is unattainable.

Childhood messages

A person's body image is created over many years, starting when they are a baby, through the constant messages they receive from parents, siblings, peers and the media. How they perceive and internalise these childhood messages determines their ability to build self-esteem and confidence in their appearance. The good news is that it is possible to change these internalised messages.

Lifestyle changes

Poor body image, low self-esteem and the fact that change is often difficult and frightening may result in individuals not making the lifestyle changes necessary to improve their overall health and body image. However, by choosing not to make the required changes, their life will continue to yield the same unsatisfactory results.

3. Improving body image

Change the way of thinking

It is not possible for a person to be happy and enjoy life if inside they are thinking sad thoughts and are unhappy or even depressed about the way they look. The solution is neither easy or quick, as it requires a change in the way they think about themselves. The first step is to be less self-critical and embrace a more sympathetic view of one's self. Rather than focussing on the aspects that they don't like, they should make an effort to list the things about themselves that they do like. Seeing their body in a positive way will improve their body image, self-esteem, general outlook and how they respond to other people.

Body distortion results in:

⇨ Emotion-based conclusions. 'I feel ugly.... therefore I must be ugly.' This thought pattern concludes that how you feel is fact.

⇨ An all-encompassing outlook. 'I have a large stomach... therefore I am unattractive.'

⇨ Focusing on the negative and ignoring the positives. 'I hate having droopy breasts.'

⇨ Altering positives to negatives. Hearing 'you look well' is interpreted as 'you have gained weight'.

It is essential to reverse the above ways of thinking and begin replacing these thoughts with positive self-affirming ones.

Self-acceptance

Transforming the way an individual thinks through positive affirmations will enable them to sympathetically accept themselves and bring the benefits of an improved outlook, e.g. 'I like myself' not 'I do not dislike myself'.

4. Changing behaviour

Often, an individual may avoid certain activities because of a poor body image. Over time, improved body image and self-esteem will result in reduced avoidance behaviour.

5. Body image and culture

Individuals who do not accept the culture 'norm' of thinness and beauty tend to have a more positive body image than those who try to achieve the 'ideal'. It is thus important to adopt a wider and more critical perspective towards society's cultural norm.

⇨ The above information is reprinted with kind permission from My Body Beautiful. Visit www.mybodybeautiful.co.uk for more information.

© My Body Beautiful

Women still aiming for size zero

More than one in five women between the ages of 18 and 24 want to be a size zero, according to a new poll

A body image survey revealed in June's *Weight Watchers* magazine also found that women struggled to identify a size zero – a size four in UK sizing – model from a line-up of six differently-sized women, with only 3% getting it right.

Out of the poll of more than 1,200 women, 900 of those surveyed estimated the size zero model as between a size 8 and 12.

Six images were presented to women for the survey, ranging from a UK size 4 (US size zero) to a UK size 26.

When asked to guess the sizes of the larger models, the women surveyed tended to underestimate, with more than half the women saying the size 26 model was one or two sizes smaller.

Londoners also seemed to prefer the thinner version, with 20% of respondents in the capital believing men find size zero women most attractive, compared with 11% in the North and Scotland.

Just 5% of women in the capital chose the size zero as the unhealthiest body shape compared with 16% of those in the Midlands and Wales.

Almost a quarter of women in these regions said men would find a size 16 the sexiest body shape but only 17% of Londoners agreed.

Mary Frances, editor of *Weight Watchers* magazine, said: 'Despite all the coverage of obesity and the size zero debate, many of us still don't recognise what is a healthy weight.

'And it's interesting to discover that location affects body image as well as house prices.'

23 April 2008

⇨ The above information is reprinted with kind permission from Sky News. Visit http://news.sky.com for more information.

© Sky News

Girls as young as seven concerned about body image

Girls between seven and ten believe being slim and pretty makes you clever, happy and popular

Girlguiding UK has today launched new research that shows girls under ten are linking body image and appearance to happiness and self-esteem. The report, *Under Ten and Under Pressure?*, has been published in partnership with leading eating disorders charity beat.

The research was carried out by pollsters Opinion Leader through a series of in-depth focus groups with girls in guiding between the ages of seven and ten. The project focused on girls of this age because many of the factors that can contribute to negative body image are now known to come into play much earlier than is generally understood – typically before girls become teenagers.

Under Ten and Under Pressure? shows the happiness and confidence of the girls who took part to be intrinsically linked to strong and supportive friendship groups, popularity, and feeling included. Their greatest fear is bullying: being singled-out, isolated or excluded.

Even at this age, weight and appearance are seen as key to securing the friendships they value so highly. Girls who are slim and pretty are seen as more likely to be happy, well-liked, friendly and clever. One participant explained: 'They're pretty and because of that they might be able to run really fast and like they're good at like reading and writing and they're good at all kind of things.' Meanwhile, girls who are overweight or less attractive are viewed as more likely to be unhappy, lonely or victims of bullying. Another girl admitted: 'If someone was a bully and they told you you look ugly and fat, then you'll go on the scales.'

Girls under ten are linking body image and appearance to happiness and self-esteem

---

There were significant differences in girls' awareness of their own weight and appearance. Some were largely unaware and unconcerned. Others described feeling overweight, anxious about wearing certain clothes, conscious of how they compare to friends and sensitive to remarks by family and friends. One girl asked: 'Am I fat? Because my brother thinks I'm fat and he always sings to me, "fatty fatty boom boom".' Another explained: 'I go to the gym nearly every day... and do sit-ups.'

Girls who live in London are the most aware and most likely to be critical of their own bodies. Other key factors are having families who comment – either positively or negatively – about appearance and having friends who have been singled out because of their weight. Girls also talked about the profound effect of even light-hearted comments, particularly from adults, about their weight and appearance. At this age, celebrities and the media have only a muted impact by comparison.

However, girls also explained that constructive and positive comments from families, friends and other supportive adults – and reminders that looks are not as important as what is on the inside – are key to countering negative thoughts about body image and appearance. Girls were much more likely to be receptive than cynical about these kinds of reassurances.

Following the research Girlguiding UK and beat formed a new self-esteem youth panel made up of representatives from Girlguiding UK's peer education programme and beat's Young Ambassadors Panel. The panel has today published a call to action for families, schools and youth organisations based on the report's findings, which includes advice for everyone to remember the potential impact of their comments about appearance and weight on young children. They have also called for more experts to be allowed into schools, for better training on eating disorders for teachers and school nurses, and for lessons that teach

And to think these are meant to be my carefree childhood years...

girls about media manipulation and airbrushing. They have advised adults to take any doubts girls express about how they look seriously – as they are often the first sign of problems that can emerge more acutely as girls grow older.

Chief Guide Liz Burnley commented on the research: 'Girlguiding UK's determination to enable girls of all ages to find the confidence they need to succeed is the reason we continue to use our girl-only space to help young women develop self-esteem through new adventures, experiences and friendships. At a time when girls and young women are under more pressure than ever before, we hope this report will shed further light on how all of us can help girls build the self-confidence and determination they need to seize the many opportunities open to them and reach their full potential.'

Girlguiding UK has also launched a new self-esteem resource for girls between 10 and 14: *Looking At Me*. The new resource covers topics from air-brushing and media manipulation to eating disorders, cosmetic surgery, celebrity role models and advertising. Building self-esteem for younger girls is also integral to the Girlguiding UK programme for girls in the younger age groups.

beat Chief Executive Susan Ringwood said: 'We were delighted to take part in this important and groundbreaking research which has clearly highlighted the concern about self-esteem and body image that today's girls feel. Eating disorders are now affecting girls as young as eight and the results of the survey serve to show just how important it is, even at this young age, to ensure they have good self-esteem. Low self-esteem and a negative body image can be high risk factors for an eating disorder developing. By building confidence and challenging negative stereotypes we know that we can help beat eating disorders.'
21 November 2007

⇨ The above information is reprinted with kind permission from Girlguiding UK. Visit www.girlguiding.org.uk for more information.
© Girlguiding UK

Celebrity culture

We look at how a celeb's appearance can affect how we feel about our own body image

Pretty unreal

A recent poll has found that 67 per cent of girls feel under pressure from celebs to have perfect bodies. With images of beautiful people everywhere, that's hardly surprising! Perfect bodies, perfect clothes, perfect hair – it's enough to make anyone feel insecure or envious and many of us spend money, time and effort trying to look just like them.

But the reality is that the media is setting up comparisons for us that are impossible to copy. What's not immediately obvious when you flick through magazines is that what you see is not all real!

Altered images

Whether you're watching music videos or looking through magazines, many of the images you're seeing are often airbrushed or enhanced.

Celebrities are in the business of looking good and they spend their money on personal trainers, hairdressers, makeup artists and designer clothes.

But even after all this effort, magazines still retouch photographs! Eyes and teeth are whitened, skin problems are covered up and hair is made to look neater and cleaner. Even images like those you see in tabloids are touched up – skin is improved, marks are gone, and all those imperfections that make someone human magically disappear! Even models who are already thin are made to look slimmer than they already are.

Body image

Seeing seemingly perfect images all the time can make you feel pretty bad about your own body. According to experts, this means that wanting to be thinner is a huge issue for many girls, while boys feel increasing pressure to be more buff.

In extreme cases girls develop eating disorders and boys can even turn to steroids in an effort to reach that goal of looking just like the unreal celebs!

Radio 1

Radio 1's advice programme 'The Sunday Surgery' recently devoted a whole programme to body image. As an experiment, breakfast presenter Chris Moyles and his team were photographed looking 'normal'. Their photographs were then retouched. The results? Everyone who knows and loves the team prefers them just the way they are – it's real!

Influence

The constant stream of perfect images everywhere can encourage you to buy products, clothes and buy into lifestyles, promoted by what seem like perfect looking celebs.

But what really makes a person look good is how they feel about themselves. If you are eating healthily, exercising regularly (but not obsessively) and feel good inside, then you will always look good on the outside too. It doesn't matter if you're short, thin, curvy or even if you don't have the right clothes, being real is what will keep you happy and looking good.

You'll find that as you get older you start to become happier and more comfortable with who you are. So starting now will mean getting to that point sooner!
13 February 2008

⇨ The above information is reprinted with kind permission from need2know. Visit www.need2know.co.uk for more information.
© Crown copyright

Body images

**Does the media put too much pressure on women to be thin?
Sophie Dyer, 16, looks at both the positive and negative messages
being sent to young people about body image**

In the last few weeks, celebrities like Courtney Love and Renée Zellweger have been criticised in the media for their dramatic weight loss.

Also, a recent BBC survey highlighted that 'half of girls aged eight to twelve want to look like the women they see in the media and six out of ten thought they'd be happier if they were thinner'.

The message that slim equals beautiful could actually end up being dangerous

As a young journalist, I wanted to get to the bottom of these shock statistics and find out the scale of this problem for myself. I went to my local shopping centre in Bexleyheath and spoke to the public to see what their opinions of this worrying trend were.

'Everyone thinks they have to look like the "perfect" person, there is no longer any emphasis on being individual.' This is the opinion of Miss Drew, a P.E. teacher with over a decade's experience of working with young people.

It seems that she has a good understanding of what young girls regard as a healthy body image. This was a theme that I found came up frequently when I asked the public, 'How much of an influence do you feel the media has over society?'

One mother I spoke to expressed her anxiety about the growing phenomenon of the media's huge influence over body image. 'I'm not sure it can be improved. I mean, how can you regulate the media? It's just a sign of the times we're living in unfortunately.' I was surprised that this issue affected such a broad section of the public, from parents to young teenagers.

Another aspect that has to be taken into consideration is the fashion industry and the influence of catwalk models. The fashion industry usually associates true beauty with being thin. Whether high street or *haute couture*, nearly all fashion outlets use slim models to advertise their collections.

What are the odds that a famous fashion designer will choose a size 16 model over a size zero? Size zero has been linked to anorexia nervosa and bulimia, as many women have to lose a large amount of weight to become so thin.

The deaths of models have even been attributed to the size zero trend. Luisel Ramos, aged 22, died of a heart attack in 2 August 2006 after apparently trying to survive on Diet Coke and lettuce leaves.

Brazilian model Ana Carolina Reston's death was also linked to the pressures of maintaining slimness; her diet was reported to consist solely of apples and tomatoes, and she died from kidney failure.

Beautiful, extravagant clothes are designed for slim people. In a society that seems so easily influenced by the media, the message that slim equals beautiful could actually end up being dangerous.

However, although celebrities and the media can be blamed for creating this problem, they could also actually provide a solution. A range of recent TV programmes have been promoting more positive attitudes towards body image.

On *How to Look Good Naked*, presenter Gok Wan encourages women to embrace their body shape; Dove's new ad campaign features larger, older and a more diverse range of models; and Coleen McLoughlin's *Real Women* also aims to promote 'real women' in fashion advertising.

Since it's been established that the media has such a dominant influence over the public, promoting and encouraging a healthy attitude towards body image may help combat these problems.

This story was written by Sophie Dyer, 16, for Headliners in partnership with Bexleyheath School.
21 July 2008

⇨ The above information is reprinted with kind permission from Headliners. Visit www.headliners.org for more information.

© Headliners

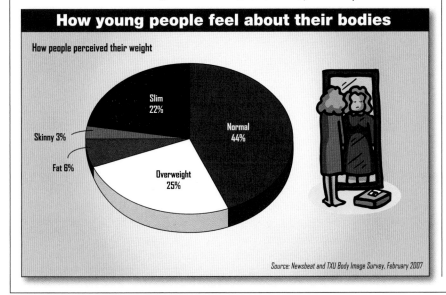

How young people feel about their bodies

How people perceived their weight

Slim 22%
Skinny 3%
Fat 6%
Normal 44%
Overweight 25%

Source: Newsbeat and TXU Body Image Survey, February 2007

Blame Mummy, not Madonna

It's not just celebrities who undermine teenage girls' self-esteem – there's a culprit far closer to home, says Elizabeth Grice

By Elizabeth Grice

Locking up our daughters is not an option. There's no such thing as a Family Fortress to keep out all the malign influences that we'd like to protect them from. Yet there can't be a parent in the country who doesn't from time to time long for some equivalent, and who doesn't feel the utter futility of trying to preserve, or at least prolong, some kind of childhood simplicity against the massed forces of consumerism and premature sexualisation that Vicky Tuck, the head of Cheltenham Ladies' College, identified at a conference this week as undermining the wellbeing of teenage girls.

Her comments reflect a pervasive anxiety among parents that children – particularly girls – are being forced to grow up too quickly because of what she calls a 'toxic cocktail' of binge drinking, social networking websites and precocious sexual expectations. 'Coarsening' is her word for it. She suggests it is exacerbated by media reports of 'Botox and bingeing'. She might as usefully and specifically have denounced teenage magazines and body-obsessed television programmes. And she would even have been correct to include parents themselves in her catalogue of unhelpful influences.

In a survey, *Under Ten and Under Pressure?*, conducted by Girlguiding UK and the Mental Health Foundation, girls as young as seven admitted to being concerned about their body image and saw weight and appearance as the key to securing the friendships they craved. But they were not as profoundly influenced by celebrities and the media as we tend to think. The comments and attitudes of their families had a much bigger part to play – both positively and negatively.

Where mothers are hung up on dieting, their daughters imbibe the same dubious values, says Deanne Jade, founder of the National Centre for Eating Disorders. 'Research shows that, again and again, parents' attitude to food, weight and shape is a powerful risk factor. They pass on their obsessions and anxieties to their children almost by osmosis. If a mother is constantly asking 'Does my bum look big in this?', it focuses a child's attention negatively and they can develop an acquired sensitivity to such things. Even fathers play a part.' In older children, such anxieties can lead to drug use and bulimia, she says.

> ## Parents' attitude to food, weight and shape is a powerful risk factor. They pass on their obsessions and anxieties to their children almost by osmosis

The stresses on children were alarmingly exposed in the Girlguiding UK report last year. Girls between 10 and 14 revealed that pressure to grow up before they were ready was overwhelming. Afraid of being singled out, isolated or excluded, they felt compelled to wear clothes that made them look older. They were confused about how to deal with sexual advances from boys and felt bombarded by magazines and websites telling them to lose weight, wear make-up and even consider plastic surgery. Two-fifths admitted to feeling worse after looking at pictures of models, pop stars or actresses. Many equated thinness and prettiness with happiness and popularity. One explained: 'When I was 11, I read a teenage magazine for the first time and that is when it kind of clicked: I should be like this.'

Simply cutting off magazines or monitoring television programmes will not stem the tide of undesirable influences and unhealthy role models, says Jade. 'It is like putting your finger in the dyke, because there is no one influence. Instead, we should try to teach them some media literacy, to show how these images are manipulated. It is a difficult and complex job and very few parents are equipped for it.'

That said, well-informed parents can help children navigate puberty, she argues. At a recent Girlguiding UK conference asking 'Is girlhood dead?', the answer was not unequivocally gloomy. 'Yes, there is a rise in binge-drinking and drug-taking,' Jade says, 'but we agreed we must not rush to panic. Girls may be exposed to undesirable influences at a younger age but they are also more resilient at a younger age. As parents and teachers, we have to keep up with that by understanding and helping them to manage the transition from childhood to adulthood with the least stress.'

⇨ The Girls' School Association, of which Vicky Tuck is president, will launch a website, mydaughter.co.uk, in January, giving parents advice on how to deal with teenage girls. At www.girlguiding.org.uk/girlsshoutout there is a 10-point Call to Action on Self-Esteem for struggling parents.

19 November 2008

Salons boom as girls yearn to grow up fast

Girls as young as six are wanting facials and manicures, and one child-only salon is now open – with dolls and DVDs as well copies of *Vogue*. But some parents worry where the trend may be heading

Seven-year-old Scout Cockayne-Francis sat in the beauty parlour chair with dignified, almost adult elegance as the beautician manicured her fingernails and painted them a soft shade of pink.

In the past she has come to Tantrum, a luxurious child-only salon in London's King's Road, to have her curly hair blow-dried and straightened, but last Wednesday morning there was just time for a 30-minute manicure before she headed off with her mother for an educational afternoon at a museum.

Tantrum, which opened as a hairdressers six months ago, has just started offering manicures and pedicures in response to demand. 'We're getting customers who come in and ask more and more whether we offer these other services,' said co-owner Latasha Malik. 'Manicures are very popular. [Parents] ask about pedicures, they ask whether we can style and blow-dry hair for young girls, have a bit of make-up put on.'

By Olivia Gordon

Malik said British parents were still 'conservative' compared to Americans. So far his youngest customer for a manicure or pedicure has been six, whereas salons in Los Angeles and New York regularly treat children as young as two.

Almost 50 per cent of girls between five and eight want to be slimmer

'Pamper-birthday' parties for young children, involving make-up, hair styling and manicures, have become commonplace in the UK, but out of this has come the demand for individual treatments, with parental consent. While Tantrum claims to be the first child-only salon, the sight of a little girl next to a grown woman

at a nail bar or spa is becoming increasingly less surprising on this side of the Atlantic.

Child beauty has become big business. Research by market analysts Mintel of 6,000 youngsters from the age of 7 to 19 found that more than six out of ten girls aged seven to ten wore lipstick and more than two in five wore eye-shadow or eye-liner. Almost one in four wore mascara and three in five wore perfume. According to a 2005 *British Journal of Developmental Psychology* study, almost 50 per cent of girls between five and eight want to be slimmer.

Recently, the launch of high heels for babies, the Miss Bimbo website, which invites users to create a virtual doll, keep it 'waif thin' with diet pills and buy it breast implants and facelifts, and padded bras for seven-year-olds sold at Tesco have all caused controversy. Last year, Barbie manufacturer Mattel announced it was teaming up with Bonne Bell cosmetics to launch a make-up line aimed at girls aged six to nine.

Children casually browse Tantrum's supply of *Tatler* and *Vogue*, watch personal DVDs and play Wii as they are preened by beauticians. The salon has Champneys hand moisturiser in the toilets, a fish tank containing stingrays in front of the basins and old-fashioned dolls with which the children can play.

'Grooming has really changed when it comes to young children. Everyone's very much aware of how they look at a very young age,' said Malik. 'They aspire to be grown up – a lot of 12- to 13-year-old girls are reading *Hello!* and *OK!* already. They bring in pictures of models, saying, "Can you do something like this?"'

Scout was brought to Tantrum from their nearby home by her mother

Andra, 39, a psychologist. Scout's friends are into beauty treatments, too, Andra said. 'At quite a young age they really enjoy the whole process of being pampered. Nearly all Scout's friends regularly get their nails done, from about the age of five. Her friends do wear eye-shadow and blusher, not at school but at parties. I don't let Scout.'

Worries about children growing up too fast are 'a dilemma' for her, Andra said. She wouldn't let Scout have her eyebrows shaped or go for a facial until her mid-teens, and sees 11 as an appropriate age to start wearing make-up.

Yet, she said, there is peer pressure for children to fit in. 'I don't want my children to be the only ones that don't experience these things. When I allow [Scout] to have her nails painted pale pink somewhere like this for a treat, it takes away that feeling of being left out.'

Scout said: 'You get to see the stingrays and it's nice. It feels quite grown up. I like to feel grown up because I'm growing older, and I like to feel older.'

The child beauty treatment trend has started to emerge outside London, too. Children as young as seven have been going for facials at the JJ Hair and Beauty Salon in St Albans. The owner, Jacqui Benjamin-Moutrie, started doing pamper

parties two years ago, and from this began to receive requests from parents for one-on-one treatments. She now only performs around 10 individual treatments per year but said: 'There is definitely a gap in the market.'

The Waterfall Spa in Leeds, too, reported that, as a result of demand, it has started mother-and-daughter days called 'Me and My Princess' that take place during the summer holidays, available to children aged between 10 and 16. Girls are offered 30-minute manicures, pedicures and facials, in addition to use of the spa facilities 'and a light lunch'.

In the US, children going to beauty salons and spas for individual treatments has been considered normal by many parents for several years, and the typical age range is significantly wider than in Britain.

The US child beauty market has snowballed in recent years, provoking controversy last April after a report in a Philadelphia magazine alluded to the bikini waxing of an eight-year-old girl in a beauty salon. A report on Good Morning America referred to nine-year-olds having chemical peels.

The Dashing Diva nail spa on Manhattan's Upper West Side is one of a number of upmarket beauty salons and spas that are now regularly treating children as young as two, one-on-one.

Four-year-old Drew Kleiner had a manicure while sitting on the lap of her mother Nina, 41, an estate agent. They were on holiday in New York and found the child beauty scene less developed than they were used to in their home city, Los Angeles.

Girls in LA start getting manicures and pedicures and wearing make-up at three, Nina said. 'It's pretty common; all Drew's friends go [to salons]. It makes them feel grown up and special.'

The child beauty hangouts in Manhattan include Cozy's chain of glamorous child hair salons, which also offer manicures, pedicures and make-up.

Jane Kantor, 43, who works in advertising, sucked a lollipop as she watched her seven-year-old daughter Caroline getting a manicure and her

hair styled at the Upper East Side branch of Cozy's on a sunny afternoon. Caroline, an after-school regular, said she wanted to look like Hannah Montana, the stage name of 15-year-old US pop idol Miley Cyrus.

Salon founder Cozy Friedman said: 'Beauty treatments have become a fun activity, a bonding thing for moms and daughters.' And it's not just girls any more, she said. 'Boys are much more conscious of their styles now. We see little boys who know exactly what they want.'

'Grooming has really changed when it comes to young children. Everyone's very much aware of how they look at a very young age'

The growing popularity of child beautification in Britain has caused concern among some parents. Sally Wray, 43, a book publicist, said: 'I recently took my three-year-old daughter to a birthday party and was horrified to see three girls from her nursery class had make-up on – it wasn't face painting, it was properly applied and blended eye shadow, blusher and lip gloss that had presumably been applied by the girls' mothers.

'It deeply disturbs me that girls are being sexualised in this way. I certainly would never take my daughter with me to a beauty salon, and I find the whole idea of little girls having beauty treatments both inappropriate and bizarre.'

Child psychologist and founder of Raisingkids.co.uk Dr Pat Spungin said: 'What are you going to be doing when you've got your nails painted at three? Are you going to be out in the garden digging for worms or in the sandpit? It's too much. It's encouraging children to become overly self-conscious and aware of their appearance. We already have enough evidence that children are feeling unhappy with themselves.'
15 June 2008

The impact of body-emphasising video games

Information from Kansas State University

Too much violence may not be the only concern with some video games. Studies conducted at Kansas State University find body-emphasising video games can negatively affect body image.

In studying violent video games, Christopher Barlett, a former K-State graduate student in psychology, and Richard Harris, K-State professor of psychology, began to notice that the characters in these games tended to have extreme body types – either very muscular males or very thin females. This observation led to a question of how the body image of individuals playing the games might be affected by these extreme body types.

> **'There's some evidence of increasing numbers of body-image disorders in men, which used to be very rare until the last 10 years or so'**

To answer that question, Harris and his research team conducted two studies.

The two study groups, made up of K-State students, were divided by gender. The men played the video game 'WWF Wrestlemania 2000,' while the women played a beach volleyball game. The participants were questioned about their body image before playing the game and then questioned again after playing the game for 15 minutes.

In only 15 minutes of playing, the game players viewed their own body images more negatively, Harris said.

'The results really weren't surprising; they were kind of what we were expecting and fulfilled one of our hypotheses,' Harris said. 'I'm not going to say that we were happy

about that, to see such an effect. It was kind of sobering that it did have such a short-term effect.'

Harris said the studies also follow a trend evolving in the media of an idealised image of men.

'There's been a lot of interest for a long time on the unrealistic supermodel image in advertising,' he said. 'What isn't as well known is that idealised masculine image is becoming so much more muscular and is just as unrealistic as the supermodel image.

'It is just as hard for the man to get his body into the shape of the WWF wrestler as it is for the woman to get her body to look like Barbie,' Harris said. 'There's some evidence of increasing numbers of body-image disorders in men, which used to be very rare until the last 10 years or so, and seems to be becoming much more common.'

For evidence of this phenomenon, Harris said to look no further than popular action figures, such as G.I. Joe, which have been bulked up in recent years, especially in comparison to their original models.

'There is no way for a man to get his body to look like those action figures without the heavy use of steroids,' Harris said. 'Everyone is aware of the female body-image problem, but what we are seeing now are males struggling

with their own kind of body-image problems.'

The study also has implications for future studies, Harris said, which could include how video games do or do not lead to objectified views of women, what the long-term effects of video games on body image are and how video games affect the body image views of the opposite gender.

Harris said the most significant thing the study showed was how immediate an impact on body image video games had.

'Video games are a part of popular culture,' he said. 'I'm certainly not saying that everyone with major body-image issues has them because of video games. That may be a part of it, but there are other factors. There may be other issues of concern with video games besides the well-known concern about violence.'
23 December 2008

⇨ Barlett earned both a bachelor's, in 2004, and a master's, in 2007, in psychology from K-State. He is now working on his doctorate in psychology at Iowa State University. The above information is reprinted with kind permission from Kansas State University. Visit www.k-state.edu for more information.

© Kansas State University

Link between lads' magazines and body image

Information from the University of Winchester

Men who regularly read 'lads' magazines' are increasingly obsessive about their body image, resulting in them doing excessive exercise and possibly taking steroids to improve their physique, according to a study by University of Winchester psychologist Dr David Giles.

Obsessive exercise to build muscular physique is a psychological condition that affects young men and has been dubbed 'Athletica Nervosa' by the media. Dr Giles' survey, published in the journal *Personality and Individual Differences*, is the first British study to explore this condition.

Heavy consumers of lads' mags think about taking anabolic steroids or use protein or energy supplements as part of their diet and exercise regimes to improve the way they look

Dr Giles, with colleague Jessica Close, surveyed 161 males aged between 18 and 36 in order to examine the influence lads' magazines have on body image and the drive for greater muscularity. Each male indicated which magazines they regularly read or brought from a list of titles including *Nuts*, *Loaded* and *FHM*, and stated their current relationship status before being scored according to their dietary habits, attitudes towards appearance and exercise regimes.

The researchers found that men who read lads' magazines, particularly single men, were more influenced by the flawless body imagery promoted by the magazines. 'The message in typical lads' magazines is that you need to develop a muscular physique in order to attract a quality mate,' says Dr Giles. 'Readers internalise this message, which creates anxieties about their actual bodies and leads to increasingly desperate attempts to modify them.'

Some of the most worrying findings were that heavy consumers of lads' mags think about taking anabolic steroids or use protein or energy supplements as part of their diet and exercise regimes to improve the way they look.

'Men and women increasingly get their ideas of what they should look like from the imagery they see in the media. The volume of content is growing and it is trapping young people in particular, into unhealthy obsessions about their own bodies,' argues Dr Giles.

The study also found differences between dating and non-dating males. 'The effect was stronger among single men than those in romantic relationships. This suggests that dating men are less anxious about their body image,' says Dr Giles. 'Although it could simply mean that they have less time to go to the gym when they have a partner.'
26 March 2008

⇨ The above information is reprinted with kind permission from the University of Winchester. Visit www.winchester.ac.uk for more information.
© *The University of Winchester*

Body dysmorphic disorder

Information from Teens First for Health

Someone with body dysmorphic disorder (BDD) is 'obsessed' with their appearance – or usually one specific bit of their body.

The condition seriously interferes with your life. It's different to the worries and wobbles which a lot of us have from time to time because it is really distressing. BDD can affect your school work, your relationships with other people, the way you dress and your mental health.

People with BDD often try and hide it, so it's hard to say how many people are affected.

It's different to the worries and wobbles which a lot of us have from time to time because it is really distressing

What causes BDD and who can get it?

There are a few theories about what causes BDD, and it probably has a number of causes rather than just one. Some experts think it's mainly biological and mostly to do with your genes. Others reckon that what you go through plays a more important role. They think that things like a difficult childhood or a really stressful experience can start BDD off.

It probably isn't either one or the other, but a combination of things – for example, the way you react to stressful situations is partly determined by your genes.

Whatever the cause, BDD makes you obsessed with a part of your body or your appearance because it seems to you that it doesn't look right or that something is wrong with it.

BDD makes you very distressed about how you look, which can seriously affect your self-esteem. You might then start doing things to try to change the way you look or to hide yourself. You might find you need to check with people that you look OK. You might also need to check your appearance in a mirror – often many times a day.

Sometimes BDD makes you avoid going out or mixing with other people because you feel so worried. This can become a vicious circle as you focus more and more on your appearance.

BDD can affect everyone. It occurs in men and women and in teenagers of both sexes. It tends to be more common in people who already have some mental health problems, for example anxiety or depression.

What are the signs and symptoms of BDD?

The condition makes you worry about a certain bit of your body. You might think it's too big or too small, or that it's out of proportion to the rest of your body. It could be anything, including the breasts and genitals or general build. But mostly it is to do with the head and neck areas, for example, nose, hair, skin, eyes, chin and lips.

You might try to hide the thing you think looks wrong with make-up or a hair cut or the type of clothes you wear. It can also take over your thoughts, so you are always checking the way you look and thinking about the thing you dislike.

Most teenagers are a bit worried about the way they look. That's not surprising when you're going through puberty and everything is changing and developing so fast. But BDD is an obsession that really interferes with your life.

People with BDD might spend a lot of time comparing themselves to people in magazines or trying to arrange their hair to get it just right. They might also pick their skin and always be asking for reassurance from other people.

How is BDD normally diagnosed and treated?

Having BDD is a very private problem and people with the condition often try to hide it. This makes getting a diagnosis tricky.

It's important that you ask for help if you think you have a problem. Speak to someone you trust, like a parent, brother or sister, close friend, teacher or doctor. They'll be able to help you get the support you need.

Treatment can have a really good impact. Cognitive behavioural therapy (CBT) is a good treatment. Here you talk your thoughts and behaviours through with someone who's trained. They will help you challenge the beliefs you have about your appearance and find ways to cope so it doesn't interfere with your life.

Speaking to a counsellor or psychotherapist could also help. But the place to start is with your doctor. They will be able to assess you and refer you to someone who can help.

You might also be given medicines, but you'll have to talk through this option with your medical team.

When to ask for help

Getting help quickly is important with BDD. This is because if left untreated, the disorder can rob you of your teenage years. If the way you think about your body is affecting your day-to-day life and making you really miserable then it's probably time to get some support.

What's going to help?

If you think you might have BDD and want to get better, there are lots of resources out there for you. Finding out a bit more about the condition and starting to read self-help books might be good.

Self-help groups can also be great – it's good to talk to other people in the same situation. You can look online or ask if there are any groups that meet in your area.

Remember that there are lots of ways to try to boost your mood.

Meeting other people or finding new interests can give you a new focus. Above all, try to stay positive and take small steps towards the bigger goal of getting better.

Looking forward

Some people living with BDD may seem to get better for a bit and then relapse. Others may stay really unwell for ages if they don't get help.

Treatment can be very effective. Being willing to accept help can really improve the outlook for most people too.

For more help and information

⇨ The mental health charity Mind is a good place to go for extra information.
⇨ The national charity OCD Action have info on BDD.
⇨ The support group BDD Central for people with OCD have information on BDD.
⇨ Visit the National Phobics Society website for loads of advice and support.
⇨ The charity First Steps to Freedom can also help with obsessions and compulsions.

13 June 2008

⇨ This article has been reproduced with kind permission from Children First for Health – Great Ormond Street Hospital's leading health information website for young people of all ages and parents: www.childrenfirst.nhs.uk

© Great Ormond Street Hospital

Lessons on the body politic

William Leith salutes a timely and powerful polemic by Susie Orbach on the western obsession with achieving physical perfection

In her first book, *Fat Is a Feminist Issue*, published 31 years ago, Susie Orbach told us why lots of women had a dysfunctional relationship with their bodies. Some women got fat, she said, not because they were greedy, but because being fat made them feel safe. For a woman, she said, being slim might get you the wrong kind of attention – not just from men, but from other women, too. So lots of people have an unconscious drive towards being fat, even if they think, on the surface, that they want to be slim. What an insight! That's what I thought, when I read it. And also: what a twisted world we live in!

As a psychotherapist, Orbach had asked women what their fat was actually doing for them. It was giving them a certain relief, they said. It 'took them out of the category of woman and put them in the androgynous state of "big girl"'. It gave them something concrete to worry about, so they wouldn't have to think about all their other troubles. 'Above all,' Orbach wrote, 'the fat woman wants to hide.'

In this new book, Orbach tells us what has happened to our bodies in the intervening three decades. These days, we live in an even more twisted world. Or, as Orbach puts it, 'the problems I sought to describe have mushroomed'. Now that we no longer use our bodies to make things, she says, we make our bodies instead. Our bodies are the product. Of course, the human body has always been sculpted by what it does. And now, mostly, it does not till the fields, or mine the coal, or hump things around. In the modern age – what Orbach calls 'late modernity' – it sits at a keyboard, tapping away, like I'm doing right now – or on a sofa, reading a newspaper, like you're doing right now.

Why, Orbach asks, 'is bodily contentment so hard to find?'

And what do sedentary people in modern societies have in common? What are we doing, exactly, when we sit at our keyboards? Well, for one thing, we're not getting much exercise. Weirdly, though, the less exercise we get, the more we worship the toned, impossible body of our dreams. But the body we dream of is always out of reach and getting harder to achieve with every passing year – for women, this body is slender body, with a certain type of breasts – and, lately, a certain type of bottom, too. For men, it's the six-pack, among other things.

So what's driving all of this? Why, Orbach asks, 'is bodily contentment so hard to find?' In her first book, she showed us how people's bodies can be shaped by forces beyond their control. Here, she turns her attention to the controlling forces – 'the merchants of body hatred'. Her point is that capitalism works much better if we hate our bodies. If we're anxious and needy, we are better consumers; if we're anxious and needy when it comes to something as fundamental as our bodies, we are putty in the hands of marketeers and diet-merchants. And if we ever start to get comfortable with what we've got, along comes another body – another piece of unattainable perfection – to keep us anxious.

Who are these merchants of hatred? Where are all these images of perfection? Actually, they're everywhere. They are, I began to think as I read this, the people sitting at the keyboards, writing the ads and marketing the holidays, airbrushing the pictures and arranging the loans. They are us, me and you, communicating, right now, via a medium partly funded by advertising. And look at the ads! Look at the bodies in the ads! And think of the meaning of those bodies, and how they got there, and what those bodies will do to us. That's one of the things I was thinking, as I was reading this book. I was thinking: it's us – it's all of us! We are the merchants of body hatred.

Orbach takes us on a world tour of body anxiety – the rock videos, the magazine covers, the ads, the people who tweak the portraits of children to make them look perfect, the high heels made for babies to wear, the mothers who diet during pregnancy, the elective caesareans, the pressure to lose 'baby weight' in new mothers, the spread of cosmetic surgery, the spread of cosmetic surgery shows... and it's all repeating the same mantra about the need, particularly for women, to be slim and sexy, but with the right breasts and now the right bottom. 'Visual muzak' she calls it.

She's right, just like she was right 31 years ago. Our bodies are being shaped by forces beyond our control and these forces are malign. She's right about cosmetic surgery – it's becoming more and more normalised and this just raises the bar, so that what looks beautiful today will look less beautiful tomorrow. She's right about the cult of celebrities. 'By creating internationally recognisable iconic figures, it appears to be inclusive and democratic,' she says. But it's not. It 'sucks out variety'. It makes us all want to look like the same few people.

And she's right about the diet industry. Did you know that, in America, the diet industry is worth $100bn a year? And the annual education budget is $127bn? And diets mostly don't work. That's because, when you go on a diet, your body gets better at sucking calories out of the food that you do eat. So when you start to eat normally again, you balloon. And that's the whole point. That's where the $100bn comes from. Diets create a need for more diets. Or,

as Orbach puts it: 'Diet companies rely on a 95 per cent recidivism rate, a figure that should be etched into every dieter's consciousness.'

But there was another voice in my head as I was reading this book about bodies. I was thinking six-packs, of clear, wrinkle-free skin, of better teeth and hair... and I secretly wanted these things. I was thinking of Brad Pitt. I was thinking of Brad Pitt's stomach. I was wondering how I could get Brad Pitt's stomach. What would life be like then? I kept thinking: I know, Susie, body tyranny is terrible. It's morally wrong and spiritually destructive. It was bad in 1978 and it's been getting worse ever since. But just imagine, all the same, a world of perfect toned slimness, in which...

Our bodies are being shaped by forces beyond our control and these forces are malign

---

I had to keep saying: wake up! She's right! And this is a terrific, timely book. Body tyranny has been hurting us for decades. At bottom, I think, it's about making us want things. Reading this book made me think: our system makes us want things until we're so damaged that we can't go on, and it's showing on our skinny, obese, scarred, tattooed, pierced and hated bodies. And now it looks like the system is breaking down. Which might be good news for bodies.

1 February 2009
© *Guardian Newspapers Limited 2009*

Susie Orbach – a life
Born
6 November 1946, London.
Educated
University of New York, Stony Brook and UCL.
Personal life
Two children with partner and fellow psychoanalyst Joseph Schwartz, from whom she recently split.
Career
1976 Founded the Women's Therapy Centre in London.
1978 Published *Fat Is a Feminist Issue.*
1981 Founded the Women's Therapy Centre Institute in New York.
1982 *Fat Is a Feminist Issue II*; and *Understanding Women: A Feminist Psychoanalytic Account* with Luise Eichenbaum.
1986 *Bittersweet: Love, Competition and Envy in Women's Relationships* with Eichenbaum.
1993 *What's Really Going on Here.*
1999 *The Impossibility of Sex.*
2001 *Susie Orbach on Eating.*
Famously treated Diana, Princess of Wales, for bulimia.
Currently a visiting professor at the LSE.
She says:
'Fat is a way of saying "no" to powerlessness and denial.'
They say:
'Virtually all feminist debate on body image and beauty imagery owes its existence to Susie Orbach's enduring formulation' – Naomi Wolf.
By Will Daunt

The unkindest cut of all

A dramatic rise in the number of teenagers opting for breast implants is concerning both parents and the medical profession. Emma Cowing finds out what's behind the disturbing trend and asks whether it can be halted

It's the must-have item among teenage girls, along with an iPod Nano and the Kate Moss at Topshop collection. But you can't buy it on the high street and it'll cost a lot more than a month's pocket money. The desperately coveted procedure? Breast augmentation.

The number of British teenagers having breast surgery has increased by more than 150 per cent in the past year according to disturbing new figures unveiled at the weekend. Statistics from three of Britain's largest cosmetic surgery chains showed that almost 600 teenagers had the surgery last year, by far the highest figure ever recorded.

In fact, such is the demand among young women for plastic surgery that there is even a new clinic, Make Yourself Amazing, aimed solely at 18- to 35-year-olds. It has signed up reality TV stars including 21-year-old Naomi Millbank-Smith, who appeared on the Channel 4 show *Shipwrecked* last year, to provide glowing testimonials about the benefits of breast augmentation.

'I have always considered breast enlargement, but after appearing on *Shipwrecked* I finally convinced myself to go through with it,' Millbank-Smith burbles, accompanied by pictures of her in a variety of bikini tops that leave little to the imagination.

> ## The number of British teenagers having breast surgery has increased by more than 150 per cent in the past year

'Being filmed for five months in a bikini is enough to make anyone think long and hard about their figure and I found myself becoming envious of the curves other girls had.'

It's not hard to see how teens are being influenced into changing their shape when the celebrities they admire are doing so.

Shami Choudhry of plastic surgery chain Transform says: 'Young women read in magazines about personalities like Chantelle (Houghton, 24, winner of 2006's *Celebrity Big Brother*, who recently went from a 32B to a 32E 'to boost my self-confidence'), who have had breast augmentations and have a great influence on teenagers.

'18- and 19-year-olds are big consumers of weekly celebrity chat titles. Every edition contains something about cosmetic surgery, and women who read these magazines often buy two or three of them a week.'

And although such procedures are still expensive, with a breast augmentation costing around £4,000-£5,000, many clinics now offer attractive payment packages, meaning a surgical operation can be paid off over many months, or even years, making it even more accessible to younger women.

Anita Naik, agony aunt and author of a number of books on teenagers, including one on the issue of self-esteem, says that she recently received a letter from a 17-year-old who had received a breast augmentation operation for her 17th birthday.

'It's seen as far more acceptable now,' Naik says. 'It's a trend. A lot of young women don't see any problem with it, though it's clearly a result of esteem issues. If a girl wants a breast enlargement in the first place, the chances are she's not happy with her body image. She'll have one either to give herself more confidence, to give herself more sex appeal, or because she thinks it will make her famous.'

Teenagers under the age of 16 cannot have plastic surgery without parental consent, and most British cosmetic surgery clinics do not operate on women under the age of 18. One cosmetic group, SurgiCare, turns away 18- and 19-year-olds and advises them to come back when they are 20.

Mark Bury, its chief executive, said: 'In some cases these women have not finished developing. Even if they have, surgery may be a knee-jerk reaction or a result of peer pressure.'

But not all cosmetic surgery chains employ the same tactics. The Hospital Group, which has 14 clinics across Britain, carried out 203 breast augmentations on 18- and 19-year-olds last year, more than doubling the number performed in 2006. The Harley Medical Group, meanwhile, which has 19 clinics nationwide, performed breast implant operations on 180 18- and 19-year-olds last year, compared with just 90 the previous year.

Christine Williamson of Silicone Support UK, which wants a total ban on silicone implants, has said in the past that she would like to see the age limit for surgery raised to 18.

'Breast implants should carry a warning saying that they can have serious implications for your health'

And she says: 'Breast implants should carry a warning saying that they can have serious implications for your health. Some of them only last for a few months, before they fold up in your body. Lots of girls go to have implants and know nothing about the possible complications. Surgeons do not have to tell them legally.'

The British Association of Aesthetic Plastic Surgeons (BAAPS) advises caution to teenagers who are contemplating plastic surgery, and urges them to speak to their doctor before considering a procedure.

Adam Searle, consultant plastic surgeon and president of BAAPS, says: 'There are obvious situations in which plastic surgery may assist a teenager with obvious deformity, for example marked asymmetry of their breast or correction of a substantial nasal deformity.

'However, the complex mix of adolescence, self-esteem, peer pressure and surgical treatments carries potential for problems.

'With the media pressures on teenagers to look good there may be an increase in requests for plastic surgery in the future.'

Naik says that those media pres-sures push teenagers to one of two extremes: 'The magazines advocate either that you have to be exceptionally skinny, like Kate Moss or Nicole Richie, or have this overly curvaceous body like a glamour model. They're both extremes, there's no in-between for normal-sized girls.'

And there are other, serious risks too. Having surgery at 18 means the patient is likely to need repeat surgery to replace the implants in later life – with the possibility of something going wrong remaining every time they go under the knife.

So with all the potential risks out there, whatever happened to the time-honoured method of investing in a decent push-up bra and some stuffing?

'There's an ethos now of doing absolutely all that you can to be as attractive as you possibly can,' says Naik. 'Whenever I go into schools or meet young women, they're always complaining about their looks and what they want to change. These days, tissue paper down your top just doesn't cut it.'

It's a worrying state of affairs for a generation of young women trying to come to terms with their own body image in a culture that is constantly hurling images of perfection at them.

And even if the age limit for breast augmentation procedures were to be raised in Britain, the likelihood is it wouldn't stop those determined to change their appearance.

'The chances are they'll just go and get the same procedure done abroad,' says Naik. 'It's not going to stop them.

'The sad truth is that nowadays, you very rarely hear a young girl say that she's happy the way she is.'

25 March 2008

© The Scotsman

Angelina Jolie's lips inspire cosmetic surgery

Cosmetic surgery experts are concerned by women who want to go under the knife in a bid to look like their favourite celebrity

According to a report in the *Sunday Telegraph*, a survey by the British Association of Aesthetic Plastic Surgeons (BAAPS) found that 'unrealistic expectations' were cited as the main reason for refusing to operate by one-third of cosmetic surgeons.

Respondents said that they often witness prospective patients who bring along a photo of the famous person they want to look like, many of whom are celebrities or glamour models.

Adam Searle, a London surgeon and former president of BAAPS, told the *Sunday Telegraph* that many women are actually more interested in achieving the famous person's lifestyle than their appearance.

He revealed: 'When a girl comes in with 150 images of models in bikinis in glamorous locations, it often turns out that the common thing isn't the shape or size of breasts, but the lifestyle in the photo shoot.

'In fact, when you unpick the psychological factors, it becomes clear that the patient may say she wants to be a D-cup but really she wants to be the girl in the lights.'

A recent poll of around 700 member surgeons of the American Academy of Facial Plastic and Reconstructive Surgery found that nearly half had recently seen patients who wanted a celebrity feature, such as Angelina Jolie's lips or Madonna's cheekbones.

5 January 2009

⇨ The above information is reprinted with kind permission from Private Healthcare UK. Visit www.privatehealth.co.uk for more information.

© Adfero Ltd

Over 34,100 aesthetic surgery procedures in 2008

Information from The British Association of Aesthetic Plastic Surgeons

The British Association of Aesthetic Plastic Surgeons (www.baaps.org.uk), the not-for-profit organisation established for the advancement of education and practice of Aesthetic Plastic Surgery for public benefit, today announced the results of their annual audit for 2008. The number of surgical procedures this year exceeds 34,100 – more than triple the amount since 2003, when 10,700 were performed. Some of the most impressive increases this year have been recorded in breast augmentation and tummy tucks (both up by 30%) and male breast reduction, which increased by a staggering 44%. The nation's brows are also on the up as male brow lifts rise by 60%.

Highlights

⇨ 34,187 surgical procedures were carried out by BAAPS members in 2008, over a 5% increase from 2007, when 32,453 were performed.

⇨ Breast augmentation was once again the most popular procedure for women with 8,439 performed (up 30% from 2007) this year.

⇨ Women had 31,183 procedures in 2008, up from 29,572 (an increase of over 5%).

⇨ Abdominoplasty (tummy tucks) also had a striking increase for both men and women with 3,638 procedures carried out, a rise of 30% from 2007, when only 2,799 were performed.

⇨ The majority of cosmetic surgery is still carried out on women (91%), while male surgery increased by over 4% with 3,004 surgical procedures carried out (2,881 in 2007).

⇨ Male breast reduction moved into the top five procedures for men (taking over from facelifts as the 5th most popular) increasing by a staggering 44% with 323 procedures this year (Only 22 were performed in 2003 – an increase of well over 1000%!)

⇨ Rhinoplasty continued to be the top procedure for men, with 698 undertaken by BAAPS members (without much of a change from 2007) but by far the most impressive percentage rise was in the number of male brow lift procedures, which went up by 60%.

⇨ Otoplasty (ear correction) increased by 23% with 1,260 procedures (up from 1,024 last year) carried out on both men and women.

According to Mr. Nigel Mercer, consultant plastic surgeon and President of the BAAPS;

'These figures indicate that despite the beginnings of a financial downturn last year, the public's interest in aesthetic surgery remained strong, especially in regards to specific procedures. Wide media coverage has helped to educate the public about the latest advances and choices available, and we are encouraged by the fact that more people are doing their research carefully and choosing reputable providers. In the current climate it is even more important that patients seeking cosmetic surgical procedures do not make decisions based on price.'

The figures in full

A total of 34,187 procedures were carried out in 2008 by BAAPS members in their private practices, compared to 32,453 in 2007. The 2008 results indicate that surgical numbers continue to grow, with a 5.4% rise over the previous year.

The top surgical procedures for men and women in 2008 were, in order of popularity:

⇨ Breast augmentation: 8,449 – up 30% from last year.

⇨ Blepharoplasty (eyelid surgery): 5,130 – down 10%.

⇨ Face/neck lift: 4,547 – up 1.7%.

⇨ Breast Reduction: 3,845 – up 13%.

⇨ Abdominoplasty: 3,638 – up 30%.

⇨ Liposuction: 3,249 – down 29%.

⇨ Rhinoplasty: 3,065 – up 1.5%.

⇨ Otoplasty (ear correction): 1,260 – up 23%.

⇨ Brow lifts: 1,004 – up 4%.

Women had 91% of all cosmetic procedures in 2008 (31,183, up from 29,572 in 2007). The top five surgical procedures for women in 2008 were: breast augmentation (8,439), blepharoplasty or eyelid

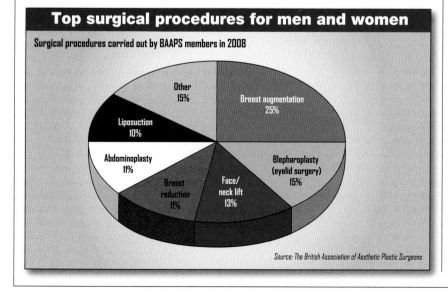

Top surgical procedures for men and women

Surgical procedures carried out by BAAPS members in 2008

- Other 15%
- Breast augmentation 25%
- Liposuction 10%
- Blepharoplasty (eyelid surgery) 15%
- Abdominoplasty 11%
- Breast reduction 11%
- Face/neck lift 13%

Source: The British Association of Aesthetic Plastic Surgeons

surgery (4,520 – down 12% on last year), face/neck lift (4,355, a rise of 2.8%), abdominoplasty or tummy tucks (3,526 – up an impressive 30.5%), and breast reduction (3,522, an increase of 11%).

Men had 3,004 cosmetic procedures in 2008 (up from 2,881 in 2007). The top five surgical procedures for men in 2008 were: rhinoplasty (698, down by 2.5%), eyelid surgery or blepharoplasty (610, an increase of 9%), ear correction or otoplasty (508, a staggering increase of 21.5%), liposuction (479, a decrease of 18%) and male breast reduction (323, an impressive rise of 44%).

According to Mr. Rajiv Grover, consultant plastic surgeon and BAAPS Secretary responsible for the UK national audit of cosmetic surgery;

'This year we have recorded a dramatic rise in a number of procedures such as male breast reduction and brow lifts. This may be due to heightened media attention, which has allowed men to realise the positive outcomes that can be achieved. It is also the first year since records began that we have seen a fall in liposuction and eyelid surgery, which may be due to the great number of non-surgical alternatives now available for those areas.'

According to consultant plastic surgeon and past President of BAAPS Douglas McGeorge;

'Those considering an aesthetic surgery should always be aware that no procedure is without risk. When performed under the right circumstances, cosmetic surgery can have a positive psychological impact and improve quality of life.'
26 January 2009

⇨ The above information is reprinted with kind permission from The British Association of Aesthetic Plastic Surgeons. Visit www.baaps.org.uk for more information.
© BAAPS

Cosmetic surgery

Information from Connexions Direct

Before you consider any cosmetic changes to your body you should be aware of the differences between plastic surgery and cosmetic surgery.

Plastic surgery is a form of skin surgery or reconstruction procedure that needs to be carried out for medical reasons and can be performed on the NHS. Plastic surgeons help people who have been disfigured from an accident or suffer because of the way they look.

Cosmetic surgery, on the other hand, is not needed for medical purposes but usually carried out for aesthetic purposes. This type of surgery is not performed by the NHS and can be expensive. Cosmetic surgery is a huge decision, as it can change your appearance forever.

Think about what you're trying to achieve. We all want to look like celebrities, but is this realistic? If you are unhappy in yourself, address your self-esteem issues before you go ahead with cosmetic surgery, as it may not make your life better in the long term.

Things to consider
⇨ Think about whether you want cosmetic surgery for the right reasons.
⇨ Talk to a parent/carer, close family member or a friend about why you are unhappy with the way your body looks. They can help you see yourself differently.
⇨ Do your research. Cosmetic surgery can be expensive and doesn't always go the way you want it to.
⇨ Talk to your Doctor/G.P. They may be able to offer other options that you might not have thought about.
⇨ Don't rush into anything. Cosmetic surgery is a life-changing decision.

Think beautiful and be beautiful
Beauty comes from the inside as well as the outside. Everyone has their ups and downs in life and we all have our 'ugly days', but remember everyone is different and it's your own features that make you special.

Learning to be happy with yourself is all part and parcel of growing up. Allow your body to develop fully before you consider changing your appearance. Sometimes all you need is a new hairstyle to boost your confidence so start with smaller, everyday changes rather than huge, dramatic changes to your body.

Who can help?
⇨ Visit the NHS web site at www.nhs.uk. You can also visit the NHS Direct website at www.nhsdirect.nhs.uk or call the NHS Direct helpline on 0845 46 47 with any problems you may have.
⇨ For more information you can also visit the Department of Health website at www.dh.gov.uk/en/Policyandguidance/Healthandsocialcaretopics/CosmeticSurgery/DH_4123795
⇨ Talk to your Doctor/G.P. as they may be able to offer other options that you might not have thought about.
⇨ You can speak to a Personal Adviser at your local Connexions Centre. To find your local centre click on the Local Services icon in the footer of the Connexions Direct homepage or check out your local phone book.
⇨ You can contact a Connexions Direct Adviser by phone on 080 800 13 2 19, by text on 07766 4 13 2 19, by textphone 08000 968 336, by adviser online or by email.

⇨ The above information is reprinted with kind permission from Connexions Direct. Visit www.connexions-direct.com for more information and advice for young people.
© Crown copyright

Cosmetic surgery: teens just 'not bovvered'

New survey reveals almost half of surgeons have registered no increase in teen enquiries

Despite recent reports in the press about teenagers allegedly turning to cosmetic surgery to either emulate celebrities or to prevent playground bullying, a survey conducted by the British Association of Aesthetic Plastic Surgeons (www.baaps.org.uk), the not-for-profit organisation established for the advancement of education and practice of Aesthetic Plastic Surgery for public benefit, found that there was little or no rise in enquiries from under 20s over the last five years. The few surgeries that did take place were to address deformities or conditions that were having a significant impact on their quality of life, such as a considerable breast asymmetry (where one breast doesn't develop at the same rate as the other, or at all), breast reduction or, most commonly, pinning back prominent ears.

> **Talking about cosmetic surgery is a long way from actually going and having it done yourself**

The survey enquired as to the amount of teenagers (patients under the age of 20) that have visited clinics for consultations in the past year, the amount that actually went through with the surgery and whether there has been an increase in interest from this age group over the last five years.

Highlights

⇨ A quarter of BAAPS surgeons have only had 0-2 consultations from patients who were under 20 years of age in the last year.

⇨ Just over a quarter (28%) of surgeons have seen between 2-5 teenage patients and the same amount (28%) have seen somewhere between 5-10 for consultations during the same period

⇨ Only one in ten saw 15 or more teenagers for consultations in the last year.

⇨ Over half (51%) of BAAPS surgeons have only operated on 0-2 teenage patients in the last year.

⇨ While less than a quarter (23%) have operated on as many as 3-5 teenage patients.

⇨ 5% of surgeons have performed cosmetic surgery on 10-15 teenagers while only 2% of surgeons have operated on over 20 teenage patients.

⇨ Just over two-fifths (43%) of surgeons have registered 'a little bit more' interest in cosmetic surgery from teenagers over the last five years, while 41% of surgeons claim there has been no increase in the same period.

BAAPS surgeons have said that if they see any teenagers at all they are normally at least 18 years of age and that the development of their body and maturity needs to be considered before moving forward with any type of surgical procedure.

According to Douglas McGeorge, BAAPS President and consultant plastic surgeon:

'There are certain situations in which plastic surgery may assist a teenager with an obvious deformity, for example marked asymmetry of their breast or correction of a substantial nasal deformity. However, surgery on a teenager should not be taken lightly – body development, maturity and self-esteem all must be considered before proceeding with such a procedure.'

Although there have been reports in the media suggesting many teens are preoccupied with breast augmentation, most surgeons have said the reality is different – the substantial majority of procedures performed on teens usually involve ear correction or breast reduction.

Rajiv Grover, Honorary Secretary of BAAPS and consultant plastic surgeon, adds:

'Considering that the number of aesthetic surgery procedures has nearly tripled in the past five years in the UK, it's natural to see an increase in interest among the public in general. However, we do not seem to have registered a particularly large change among teenagers – the few I see tend to want ear correction, or very occasionally, rhinoplasty.'

According to Douglas McGeorge:

'Lots of kids may talk about it, but talking about cosmetic surgery is a long way from actually going and having it done yourself.'

28 August 2008

⇨ The above information is reprinted with kind permission from the British Association of Aesthetic Plastic Surgeons. Visit www.baaps.org.uk for more information.

© BAAPS

Has the press exaggerated teenage cosmetic surgery procedures?

Love your body

Information from Channel 4

There's something wrong with a world that doesn't show how beauty, courage and intelligence can come in many shapes and sizes,' says AdiosBarbie, a website dedicated to helping people of any size, shape or colour improve the way they feel about themselves.

'My body is the way it is'

Having a poor body image – your mental picture of the way you look – is a common problem, made worse by the proliferation of 'perfect' body images in the media. The concern isn't just a female worry, either. One man talking on the AdiosBarbie website says, 'After a long time believing I run, lift, bike, hike and try to "eat right" in the interest of being fit, I've realised my motivations are more superficial than healthy. I worry about what I'm convinced I should look like, based on magazines and movies.'

It is possible to change the way you think about your body. Being unhappy or dissatisfied because your body image doesn't match the often impossibly high ideals of airbrushed supermodels or film stars is tough on your self-esteem, and can make you feel that it's not worth the effort of trying to make changes. It can also have you abandoning good intentions completely if you slip up just once on a diet or exercise plan. Thinking patterns can be unlearned, like any other habit, and the more often you think upbeat about yourself, the more easily negative thoughts will fade into the background.

Some of the following techniques will help you create a positive mindset, but if worries about your weight or body are getting you down, there are many places where you can get sympathetic and professional help.

Get a better body image

⇨ Dr Susan Jeffers, author of *Feel the Fear and Do It Anyway*, recommends affirmations as a powerful tool to altering your mindset. 'Every morning, look in the mirror and repeat a positive thought about yourself out loud several times: "I look great, just the way I am", "I am powerful and efficient", "I am creative and strong". Don't worry if you feel crazy at first. Keep saying it, and very soon you'll find you believe it.'

Treating your body as worthy of love and respect is an important aspect of healthy self-esteem

---

⇨ Nutrition consultant Lyndel Costain suggests these techniques: 'Think of six things you really like about your appearance – your smile, your eyelashes, your fingers. Remind yourself of these, whenever negative thoughts about other parts of your body start creeping in. "I may not be so keen on my thighs, but I've got fantastic ankles!" Or ask a friend to list four or more things that they think are good about your appearance. You'll almost certainly be pleasantly surprised to find how differently they view your body from the way you see it. And finally, if someone says you look good, don't shrug off the compliment. Take it as meant, and say thanks.'

⇨ 'Don't surround yourself with images of people you could never look like,' says AdiosBarbie. 'Create a wall of inspiration with pictures of... friends and family who love and support you.'

⇨ 'Look after yourself,' advises psychotherapist Linda Tschirhart Sanford. 'This is especially important if you spend a lot of time taking care of others, and tend to neglect yourself. Treating your body as worthy of love and respect is an important aspect of healthy self-esteem. Whatever makes you feel good, whether it's dancing, having your hair done, having a lie-in, going to the movies, resolve to do it, and do it often. Remind yourself frequently that you are far, far more than just a body. The essential you is an amalgam of so many things: your imagination, your sense of humour, the way you express yourself, your talents. All your unique qualities, of which your body is just one, combine to make you what you are.'

⇨ The above information is reprinted with kind permission from Channel 4. Visit www.channel4.com for more information.

© Channel 4

Improve body image

Information from Disordered Eating

For most of us, there are things we do not like about our physical appearance, such as our weight and body shape. These things can often get us down. So what can we do to improve our body image perception and feel more confident about ourselves?

Practice self-affirmations

Self-affirmations are positive statements about yourself that you repeat aloud on a daily basis. Write them down on pieces of paper; stick them on the mirror, on the fridge, on your desk, by the bed, even under your pillow – anywhere they will get your attention, and when they do, read them out loud.

Even if you don't believe the statements are true at first, eventually they will trickle into your sub-conscious and become part of your reality, helping you to overcome any negative feelings you have about yourself. It is important you start and end each day with a positive affirmation. Here are some examples:

⇨ 'I am going to feel good about myself all day.'
⇨ 'I feel very happy about the way I look.'
⇨ 'I have many things to be proud of in my life.'
⇨ 'Today I am going to achieve all the things I want to.'
⇨ 'My body is healthy, strong and functioning well.'
⇨ 'I can't wait for the next challenge in my life.'
⇨ 'I am going to eat healthily and exercise often to improve my health.'

Ditch the scales

You only need to monitor your weight if your health is at risk from being underweight or overweight, in which case your health care provider should take care of it. If you cannot resist the urge to hop on the scales, remember these points:

⇨ There is no 'one' perfect weight. There is no point in trying to achieve something that doesn't exist.
⇨ Weight fluctuates depending on the time of day, when you last ate, time of the month, etc, so what's the point?
⇨ Ditching the scales will help stop you being so hung up about your weight – if you can't weigh yourself, you won't know what it is!
⇨ The scales don't really tell you anything helpful; in fact most of the time they make you feel disappointed. Before scales were invented, people couldn't weigh themselves – and they coped!

Remember, images in magazines and on television are not real

Stop comparing yourself to people with so-called 'perfect' bodies in magazines and on television. It is unrealistic to expect to look like them, in fact it is unlikely you will ever look like them – no one will because it's just not possible!

For one thing, fashion models are not representative of the population. Quite often they are stick thin and of an unhealthy weight, possibly suffering from eating disorders themselves in order to keep their weight down and get work. Clever camera angles, good lighting, expert make-up and airbrushing are used to get that image of 'perfection'.

It's just not real; no one gets out of bed looking like that. Similarly, the bulging muscles seen in men's fitness magazines are unobtainable for most men, unless of course they are prepared to spend five hours a day in the gym and make use of anabolic steroids.

High profile, 'perfect' looking actors on television have a team of people to cook for them, train them to get into shape, do their make-up and hair and so on, otherwise they wouldn't be able to look the way they do. Like models, they face huge pressure to look a certain way in order to get work.

For the rest of us 'normal' people, let's stop trying to look like these people. Let's concentrate on enjoying real life and the things that really matter; it's simply not worth wasting our energy on things that don't.

Focus on your health

Your body is a fine piece of machinery with astounding capabilities. Think about what you do for it in return. Does it really deserve the constant battering about not being good enough? Does it really deserve to have so much negativity directed at it?

Why are we worrying so much about the way we look when there are more serious matters to attend to – cancer, heart disease, diabetes, obesity; these are all things that pose an immediate threat to health, yet we are more worried about the image we see in the mirror.

Learn to appreciate your body and concentrate on looking after it and keeping it healthy. If you give your body healthy foods and regular exercise, it will reward you a hundred times over by becoming fitter, stronger and more efficient than ever before.

⇨ The above information is reprinted with kind permission from Disordered Eating. Visit www.disordered-eating.co.uk for more information.
© Disordered Eating

Link between teenage girls' self-esteem and sport

Information from the Coca-Cola Company

Following comments from Ed Balls, Secretary of State for Children, Schools and Families, who was voicing concerns over the 'real issue with girls in secondary schools' not wanting to take part in sport, a survey from 'Minute Maid' Schools Cup last year reveals those football-playing teenage girls are likely to have a better body image, be healthier and more confident than their less active friends.

Football-playing teenage girls are likely to have a better body image, be healthier and more confident than their less active friends

---

One in twenty (17 per cent) of those who have never taken part in a football game think a size eight or smaller is a healthy body shape and, worryingly, it's size zero super waif Keira Knightley's body that they most admire. Yet footie players put curvy WAG Coleen McLoughlin and yummy mummy Davina McCall as the celebrities with the most enviable bods.

In fact, nearly three-quarters (70 per cent) of footie-loving girls rate their confidence as high or average, with 84 per cent of all girls stating playing sports means teenagers have a healthier attitude to life, as well as a healthier body image.

The survey of 1,250 UK teenage girls and women by the 'Minute Maid' Schools' Cup in May 2007 revealed that two-thirds of people (66 per cent) even think girls who play football in their youth make higher achievers later on in life and more than 60 per cent of people think playing team

sports can help women progress further in their career.

Fiona Hunter, independent nutritionist, comments: 'With such a lot of pressure on teenage girls to pursue unrealistic diets, I wholeheartedly support any initiative that helps them become more confident about their body image. The research clearly shows that playing team sports such as football is positive for young girls' self-esteem and confidence and has a direct relation to how they view their body image.'

And it's good to see that football-playing girls are on the up. 72 per cent of girls aged 19-21 have played team football before, plus more than three-quarters (77 per cent) of girls state they would choose to play football over netball if they had the choice. This corresponds with the FA, which states that football has become the top sport for girls and women in the country with 1.5 million girls under the age of 15 playing some form of football over the past 12 months.

Jane Ludlow, captain of Arsenal's victorious ladies' team (which secured a historic quadruple win – the FA Cup, UEFA Cup, Premier League and Premier League Cup) and captain of the Welsh national team, comments: 'It is great to see such a rise

in interest in women's football over the past few years. We have a great youth development team and I have also noticed the pressure that these girls are often under to conform to skinny celebrities. We work hard to improve their confidence and self-esteem levels, as not only does this have an impact on how they perform on the pitch, but also improves their happiness in all aspects of their lives.'

The survey also reveals:

⇨ Nearly half of those (47 per cent) who have played football think that size 10-12 is their idea of a healthy woman's figure.

⇨ 88 per cent think football is a good choice of sport to help teenagers improve vital team skills, confidence and fitness levels.

⇨ Nearly a quarter (22 per cent) of footie fans found improved confidence levels which helped them to have fun and meet new people.

30 January 2008

⇨ The above information is reprinted with kind permission from the Coca-Cola Company. Visit www.thecoca-colacompany.com for more information.

⇨ The word 'esteem' is derived from the Latin word which means 'to estimate'. As such, identifying whether or not we are suffering from low or high self-esteem can be established by focusing on how we 'estimate' or view ourselves. (page 1)

⇨ Having good self-esteem doesn't mean being arrogant or big-headed; it's about believing in yourself, and knowing that although you might not be perfect, you're still a valuable, unique human being. (page 3)

⇨ A survey of 2,004 16- to 25-year-olds conducted by YouGov on behalf of the Prince's Trust found that 14% of young people felt that life had no purpose and 10% felt life was not worth living. For young people not in education, employment or training, 27% felt that life had no purpose. (page 4)

⇨ Confidence can refer to how we feel about ourselves and our abilities, whereas self-esteem refers directly to whether or not we appreciate and value ourselves. (page 8)

⇨ Children base their self-esteem on the opinions they feel other people have of them. A child who gets positive vibes from his/her parents and other people in society will grow up feeling loved, cared for and have high self-esteem. (page 9)

⇨ According to research by a psychology professor from the University of Georgia, those with 'secure' high self-esteem are less likely to be verbally defensive than those who have 'fragile' high self-esteem. (page 13)

⇨ Psychologists from the Open University have found that children aged eight and nine had high levels of self-esteem and optimism, but this dipped in adolescence. Sixteen and 17-year-olds had the lowest levels of self-esteem (page 16)

⇨ Body image has to do with how you think about your size and shape. How you think about your body relates to how you think about yourself as a whole, so a negative body image is often linked to low self-esteem, anxiety, depression and feeling bad about yourself. (page 17)

⇨ An Ofsted survey of almost 150,000 children aged 10 to 15 found that 32 per cent of pupils worry about their bodies. (page 17)

⇨ *Bliss* magazine asked 2000 girls, aged between 10 and 19, how they felt about their bodies. Nine out of ten confessed they weren't happy with how they looked and two-thirds thought they needed to lose weight. (page 18)

⇨ More than one in five women between the ages of 18 and 24 want to be a (US) size zero, according to a poll from *WeightWatchers* magazine. (page 20)

⇨ Research from GirlGuiding UK shows that girls under ten are linking body image and appearance to happiness and self-esteem. (page 21)

⇨ A recent BBC survey highlighted that 'half of girls aged eight to twelve want to look like the women they see in the media and six out of ten thought they'd be happier if they were thinner'. (page 23)

⇨ Research by market analysts Mintel of 6,000 youngsters from the age of 7 to 19 found that more than 6 out of 10 girls aged 7 to 10 wore lipstick and more than two in five wore eye-shadow or eye-liner. (page 25)

⇨ A study from Kansas State University found that after playing a body-emphasising video game for just 15 minutes, game players viewed their own body images more negatively. (page 27)

⇨ Men who regularly read 'lads' magazines' are increasingly obsessive about their body image, resulting in them doing excessive exercise and possibly taking steroids to improve their physique, according to a study by University of Winchester psychologist Dr David Giles. (page 28)

⇨ Someone with body dysmorphic disorder is obsessed with their appearance – or usually one specific bit of their body. (page 29)

⇨ The number of British teenagers having breast surgery increased by more than 150 per cent between 2007 and 2008. (page 32)

⇨ The number of surgical procedures in 2008 exceeded 34,100 – more than triple the amount since 2003, when 10,700 were performed. (page 34)

⇨ The majority of cosmetic surgery is carried out on women (91%), while male surgery increased by over 4% in 2008. (page 34)

⇨ A survey conducted by the British Association of Aesthetic Plastic Surgeons found that there was little or no rise in enquiries from under-20s over the last five years. (page 36)

⇨ Football-playing teenage girls are likely to have a better body image, be healthier and more confident than their less active friends, according to a survey from 'Minute Maid'. (page 39)

GLOSSARY

Affirmations
Positive statements which may be used by someone suffering from low self-esteem to help change their attitude: for example, 'I am a determined individual capable of achieveing my goals.'

Assertiveness
Assertiveness is a way of expressing yourself in a direct, honest and appropriate way. An assertive person can effectively communicate with other people without being either passive or aggressive.

Blepharoplasty
Cosmetic surgery which changes the appearance of the eyelids. This accounted for 15% of surgical procedures carried out by BAAPS members in 2008.

Body dysmorphic disorder
Someone with body dysmorphic disorder (BDD) is 'obsessed' with their appearance, or one specific bit of their body. The condition is different to normal worries everyone has about their bodies as it interferes with your life and is very distressing. BDD can affect your school work, your relationships with other people, the way you dress and your mental health.

Body image
Your body image is your mental picture of the way you look. How you think about your body relates to how you think about yourself as a whole, so a negative body image is often linked to low self-esteem and can lead to anxiety and depression.

Cosmetic/aesthetic surgery
Cosmetic or aesthetic surgery refers to a non-essential surgical procedure for the purpose of improving your appearance.

Eating disorders
Eating disorders are a group of mental health disorders that interfere with normal eating habits. They can lead to serious health problems and, in the case of both Bulimia Nervosa and Anorexia Nervosa, even death. Individuals suffering from an eating disorder often have a distorted body image.

Liposuction
A form of cosmetic surgery which extracts excess fat from under the skin. This accounted for 10% of surgical procedures carried out by BAAPS members in 2008.

Otoplasty
Cosmetic surgery which changes the appearance of the ears.

Rhinoplasty
Cosmetic surgery which changes the appearance of the nose.

Self-esteem
The word 'esteem' is derived from the Latin word which means 'to estimate'. Self-esteem can be described as the way we view ourselves, how we value ourselves or how much we like ourselves.

Self-perception
An awareness of your own characteristics and personality.

Size zero
Size zero refers to a UK size 4 (size zero in the US) and is often referred to in the debate surrounding extreme thinness. Some fashion shows have now banned size zero models from the catwalk to counter claims that they are bad role models for young people and could be responsible for a rise in eating disorders.

INDEX

Additional Resources

Other Issues *titles*

If you are interested in researching further some of the issues raised in *Body Image and Self-Esteem*, you may like to read the following titles in the **Issues** series:

⇨ Vol. 174 *Selling Sex* (ISBN 978 1 86168 488 2)

⇨ Vol. 165 *Bullying Issues* (ISBN 978 1 86168 469 1)

⇨ Vol. 162 *Staying Fit* (ISBN 978 1 86168 455 4)

⇨ Vol. 142 *Media Issues* (ISBN 978 1 86168 408 0)

⇨ Vol. 141 *Mental Health* (ISBN 978 1 86168 407 3)

⇨ Vol. 139 *The Education Problem* (ISBN 978 1 86168 391 5)

⇨ Vol. 136 *Self-Harm* (ISBN 978 1 86168 388 5)

⇨ Vol. 127 *Eating Disorders* (ISBN 978 1 86168 366 3)

⇨ Vol. 125 *Understanding Depression* (ISBN 978 1 86168 364 9)

⇨ Vol. 124 *Parenting Issues* (ISBN 978 1 86168 363 2)

⇨ Vol. 121 *Young People and Health* (ISBN 978 1 86168 354 0)

⇨ Vol. 100 *Stress and Anxiety* (ISBN 978 1 86168 314 4)

For more information about these titles, visit our website at www.independence.co.uk/publicationslist

Useful organisations

You may find the websites of the following organisations useful for further research:

⇨ **The British Association of Aesthetic Plastic Surgeons:** www.baaps.org.uk

⇨ **beat:** www.b-eat.co.uk

⇨ **British Psychological Society:** www.bps.org.uk

⇨ **Care for the Family:** www.careforthefamily.org.uk

⇨ **Connexions Direct:** www.connexions-direct.com

⇨ **Disordered Eating:** www.disordered-eating.co.uk

⇨ **Dove Self-Esteem Fund:** www.campaignforrealbeauty.co.uk

⇨ **Family Matters Institute:** www.familymatters.org.uk

⇨ **Girlguiding UK:** www.girlguiding.org.uk

⇨ **Headliners:** www.headliners.org

⇨ **La Belle Foundation:** www.selfesteem.org

⇨ **My Body Beautiful:** www.mybodybeautiful.co.uk

⇨ **need2know:** www.need2know.co.uk

⇨ **The Prince's Trust:** www.princes-trust.org.uk

⇨ **Psychologies:** www.psychologies.co.uk

⇨ **Shining Bright:** www.shining-bright.co.uk

⇨ **Teens First for Health:** www.childrenfirst.nhs.uk

⇨ **TheSite:** www.thesite.org

⇨ **Uncommon Knowledge:** www.uncommon-knowledge.co.uk

ACKNOWLEDGEMENTS

The publisher is grateful for permission to reproduce the following material.

While every care has been taken to trace and acknowledge copyright, the publisher tenders its apology for any accidental infringement or where copyright has proved untraceable. The publisher would be pleased to come to a suitable arrangement in any such case with the rightful owner.

Chapter One: Self-Esteem

What is self-esteem?, © Shining Bright, *Self-esteem*, © beat, *Do you sometimes wish you were someone else?*, © Care for the Family, *How do you really feel about yourself?*, © Dove Self-Esteem Fund, *'Soft skills' for low self-esteem*, © Uncommon Knowledge, *Recognise your negative thinking patterns*, © MSN, *Learn how to be your own best friend*, © Telegraph Group Limited, *Confidence and self-esteem*, © University of Wolverhampton, *Building your child's confidence and self-esteem*, © FMI, *Assertiveness*, © TheSite.org, *How do other people see you?*, © Psychologies, *High self-esteem not always what it's cracked up to be*, © University of Georgia, *Can we teach people to be happy?*, © Guardian Newspapers Limited, *Psychologists research the rollercoaster of life*, © British Psychological Society.

Chapter Two: Body Image

Teens and body image, © About.com, *Mirror image*, © Great Ormond Street Hospital, *Problems and improvement*, © My Body Beautiful, *Women still aiming for size zero*, © Sky News, *Girls as young as seven concerned about body image*, © Girlguiding UK, *Body image*, © Headliners, *Blame Mummy, not Madonna*, © Telegraph Group Limited, *Salons boom as girls yearn to grow up fast*, © Guardian Newspapers Limited, *The impact of body-emphasising video games*, © Kansas State University, *Link between lads' magazines and body image*, © University of Winchester, *Body dysmorphic disorder*, © Great Ormond Street Hospital, *Lessons on the body politic*, © Guardian Newspapers Limited, *The unkindest cut of all*, © The Scotsman, *Angelina Jolie's lips inspire cosmetic surgery*, © Adfero Ltd, *Over 34,100 aesthetic surgery procedures in 2008*, © BAAPS, *Cosmetic surgery*, © Crown copyright is reproduced with the permission of Her Majesty's Stationery Office, *Cosmetic surgery: teens just 'not bovvered'*, © BAAPS, *Love your body*, © Channel 4, *Improve body image*, © Disordered Eating, *Link between teenage girls' self-esteem and sport*, © The Coca-Cola Company.

Photographs

Flickr: pages 7 (Sarah G); 26 (Cristee Dickson); 36 (aesop).
Stock Xchng: pages 14 (Zeeshan Qureshi); 28 (Brian Lary); 38 (Tara Bartal).

Illustrations

Pages 2, 16, 25, 31: Simon Kneebone; pages 6, 18, 27, 32: Don Hatcher; pages 9, 21, 28 39: Angelo Madrid; pages 15, 37: Bev Aisbett.

Editorial and layout by Claire Owen, on behalf of Independence Educational Publishers.

And with thanks to the team: Mary Chapman, Sandra Dennis, Claire Owen and Jan Sunderland.

Lisa Firth
Cambridge
May, 2009